# "I Will Build MY Church"
## -JESUS CHRIST

Joe Durso with Greg Treat

*To our Lord and Savior Jesus Christ, who alone is the creator of all things, by whose sufferings He is head of His Church, and without whom we would have no reason to write this book.*

# CONTENTS

# Acknowledgments

To John MacArthur, by the grace of God, a rare and extraordinary Biblicist, who consistently set before me what the Bible says and never questioned the plain truth of what is revealed in its pages. Furthermore, by his teaching, if I follow the correct means of interpreting God's meaning in what is written, I should not let my opinion or that of any other man deter me from understanding it. Lastly, to walk in humility by not straying from the orthodoxy of past generations of God's people used to perpetuate an unchanging Gospel message.

To everyone, by their example, who has set before me an unwillingness to yield in the face of strong opposition and preferred to be hurt or ostracized rather than compromise their convictions concerning the building of Jesus Christ's Church.

To my wife, thank you for your loyalty, which strengthened me over many years and through many difficulties. She stood by me even when problems arose when church building became a burden rather than a joy because of disagreements with leaders on various topics.

# FOREWORD

What does it take to write a book about an institution inaugurated fifty days after the resurrection of Jesus Christ, scattered across the planet's surface, and as divided as the world's religions? To be done well, a book about the church can only be written by devotion to the scriptures, a death to selfish ambition, undue admiration for men usurping authority over the Bible, and a teachable spirit that can only be attained by death at the cross of Jesus Christ.

No person looking through the lens of what sinful flesh can distort, demonic deception can deceive, and improper motivations can mislead can say, I'm worthy of writing about the church of Jesus Christ. Therefore, the first inclination might be that no one should write about the church. It's like Moses at the burning bush, "Lord send whomever You will" with the unspoken words, "...but not me." Then the burning bush becomes an internal fire that will not be quenched, and from down deep inside, where the Holy Spirit resides, comes the words, "Proclaim the truth, and I will lead you."

Greg and I will leave it up to our readers to decide if the words herein are faithful to scripture or based on personal prejudice. We only ask the reader to do serious soul-searching concerning their opinions. It only matters what God has written and not what we interpret. If our interpretations are consistent with God's law and will, it becomes what God has written as if we weren't involved. It is our prayer that God be glorified, our names be forgotten, and the church will accomplish God's purposes.

To these ends, be blessed by the reading of this book.

# Preface

## Continual Warnings to the Church

How should we feel when a man living 125 years ago devoted his life and work to knowing and proclaiming Christ's Gospel first from his knees and then with his mouth says the following?

"Devotion is the particular frame of mind found in one entirely devoted to God ...it is foreign to everything like lightness of spirit, and is opposed to levity and noise and bluster ...devotion belongs to the devout man, whose thoughts and feelings are devoted to God ...God dwells where the spirit of devotion resides ...Without devotion, a prayer is an empty form, a vain round of words."

Sad to say, much of this kind of prayer prevails today in the Church. Ours is a busy age, bustling and active, and this bustling spirit has invaded the Church of God. There are many religious performances. The Church works at religion with the order, precision, and force of real machinery. But too often, it works with the heartlessness of machinery.

There is much treadmill movement in our ceaseless round and routine of religious doings. We pray without praying. We sing without singing with the spirit and the understanding. We have music without the praise of God being in it or near it. We go to Church by habit and come home all too gladly, when the benediction is pronounced. We read our accustomed chapter in the Bible, and feel quite relieved when the task is done. We say our prayers by rote, as a schoolboy recites his lesson, and are not sorry when the amen is uttered.

Religion has to do with everything but our hearts. It engages our hands and feet, it takes hold of our voices, it lays its hands on our money, it affects even the posture of our bodies, but it does not take hold of our affections, our desires, our zeal, and make us serious, desperately in earnest, and cause us to be quiet and worshipful in the presence of God."

The Essentials of Prayer, E.M. BOUNDS, Start Publishing LLC, pg. 170-173

It is possible to build God's Church without God, at least in appearance. There are many such churches today; they are Christian in name only. Such a thought is revealed to us by the prophet of God, Jeremiah. "I did not send these prophets, but they ran. I did not speak to them, but they prophesied. But if they had stood in My council, then they would have announced My words to My people, and would have turned them back from their evil way and from the evil of their deeds." (Jeremiah 23:21, 22)

I Will Build My Church is not meant for only one group of Christians. There are churches entirely without God; our hearts cry for them and hope they will heed the sentiments written herein. Furthermore, very well-meaning Christians should know what is missing from their worship.

Edward McKendree Bounds lived from 1835 to 1913, but his words and thoughts are most relevant today. He spoke from the heart about the condition of the heart in those who practice religion. It is all too easy to backslide, lose our first love, and become lukewarm regarding the importance of our faith and practice. James, speaking to the twelve tribes dispersed abroad, said, "From the same mouth come both blessing and cursing. My brethren, these things ought not to be this way" (James 3:10).

God's people should be one in their minds and hearts and not divided to serve God and the world. The world is proud and petty, boastful, and lacking any humility; its leaders are tyrannical and with little to no concern for those they lead. The world is filled with people who say they know God but denounce Him with their actions. Religious worship can be formal and dull or loud and sensational but, in either case, unacceptable to God.

Building the Church is God's business, which He has entrusted to His beloved, qualified, and very capable Son. Jesus said, "…I will build My Church; and the gates of Hades will not prevail against it" (Matthew 16:18). Death itself cannot stop Jesus from building His Church.

Christ is sovereign, which means He is in complete control and has the ultimate purpose behind the things that are not in perfect accord with His revealed will. This purpose does not excuse His people's disobedience; however, disobedience results in the Church when His people cooperate with the world, the flesh, and the devil.

## 1200 Years of Israel's Disobedience

There is nothing vague about God's divine will as set forth on the Old Testament pages in the first four books of the Bible. The history of Israel reveals the disobedience of a people who did not submit to God's will. From the beginning, Israel had no faith in God in light of Egypt's destruction right before their eyes. The unregenerate have no faith in God because only a repentant sinner who is united with God by faith in His Christ can become a child of God.

The nation of Israel was lost spiritually, though saved from slavery in Egypt. God saved the remnant in Israel. Jesus said, "For the gate is narrow and the way is constricted that leads to life, and there are few who find it" (Matthew 7:14). Many took pride in their "birthright" as Hebrews, thinking themselves to be in the kingdom of God because they were the children of Abraham but were not. Many build on the sands of self-deception and phony religion only to learn they're not getting into the kingdom at the final Judgment but go to hell.

# A Prechurch Warning

The first chapter in the book of Acts records the actions of men sent out by Jesus Christ, having received many proofs of His resurrection and command to wait in Jerusalem for what the Father had promised, the filling of the Holy Spirit of power and discernment. They did wait and pray except for one solitary action.

The account of the Apostles choosing a man to take the place of Judas is not in scripture to fill space. Twelve names are written on the twelve foundation stones of the New Jerusalem, not thirteen, just twelve. Pentecost had not yet occurred, and neither had the Holy Spirit's power and influence exercised in them. Their actions were done in the flesh, premature, and not in the will of God. Of all things, it was choosing a man who would become an Apostle.

There are 12 Apostles, and that ministry distinction is now closed. The Apostle Paul, by the authority of scripture, declares him to be an apostle repeatedly throughout the New Testament. Peter and the eleven erred by appointing Matthias to the office by picking lots before the time of the Apostle Paul. The practice of picking lots is never again seen in the New Testament.

As the scriptures declare concerning the priesthood in Hebrews 5:4-5, "And no one takes the honor to himself, but receives it when he is called by God, even as Aaron was. So also Christ did not glorify Himself to become a high priest, but He who said to Him, "YOU ARE MY SON, TODAY I HAVE BEGOTTEN YOU."

God's will for the Church today is that God chooses every believer and calls them to minister according to His revealed design and without the unappointed assistance of worldly, fleshly, and proud leaders. Church leaders often tend to assume authority that belongs to Christ alone. The Apostle Paul did not wait for the eleven's approval to preach the Gospel, plant churches, and disciple men. He just did it! I can hear leaders say, but he was an Apostle. That is true, but he was also the blueprint, not for Apostleship that belongs to the 12 alone, but for calling.

When called to ministry, Martin Lloyd Jones was not readily accepted by the clergy of his day. His ministry to his first and second churches and the world stands like a beacon to all those called by God, regardless of what the clergy says. The same could be said about numerous men throughout the last 2,000 years.

Christians who believe in Jesus Christ while living for and like the world are a pitiful testimony of the Church. Authentic Christians are tempted by the world, the flesh, and the devil and agonize against it. The Apostle Paul, when writing to the Corinthian believers, said, "For the kingdom of God is not in words, but in power" (1 Corinthians 4:20).

As he once wrote, Paul understood, "For I am not ashamed of the gospel of Christ: for it is the power of God to salvation to everyone that believes" (Romans 1:16). However, words can be empty when they only go skin deep. Man believes from the heart unto salvation, or else he remains lost. In the 19th Century, multitudes left their native shores out of obedience to Christ, many to never see them again, to bring the Gospel to those who had never heard it. Theirs were not empty words.

There is a way for the Church to live out its existence that turns death into life, sin into righteousness, and dishonor into glory. Therein lies the theme of this book when the Church integrates the Old Testament law, not ordinances that reflect the law fulfilled in Christ, but the law as a principle and means of separation from the world. It is no longer to be dietary regulations that separate God's people from the surrounding nations but the presence of the Holy Spirit's fire at the cross that consumes the works of the flesh that would be conceived by association with the world and its ways.

Christians should always strive to be complete. Completeness is a word that belongs to God alone. It is to God's glory when a person leaves to be a missionary and fulfill The Great Commission. However, whether on native or foreign soil, it takes more than travel and words to fulfill the will of God.

I Will Build My Church is a book to help clarify what it means to be in the world and not of it.

# Introduction

A man can be the CEO of the largest company in the world, in the chief position of importance, and still not own the business. Such a person is always subject to review and can be terminated. However, such a man could be adopted and be in line to inherit the family business.

In Christianity, there is only one God. No one can ever move into His position or replace Him. There is one creator; everyone owes the entirety of their life to Him. Men can inherit the Kingdom, but they can never replace the king.

The book I WILL BUILD MY CHURCH is about understanding the difference between authority and designated authority. God alone possesses ultimate authority; men are always responsible for obeying God's will. Peter, as an Apostle, was given the keys to the Kingdom. He received the keys from God; they are Christ's keys. Peter and all who follow in his steps can only bind what is already bound in heaven. Today, no preacher, pastor, elder, or member has authority apart from what he receives.

God alone possesses authority and power inherently. There is the authority to make decisions and the power to make them happen. Apart from God's power, men can receive commands but never be able to carry them out. I can not walk one step by my strength unless God makes it happen. "The God who made the world and all things in it ...is not served by human hands ...since He Himself gives to all people life and breath and all things ...for in Him we live and move and have our being" (Acts 17:24-25, 28).

We need to consider carefully the One that stands at the center of the universe. The same presides over the Church. Men can manufacture a Church building and bring people into it for one reason or another. However, on the final day, men will fully understand just how little they played a part in building Christ's Church.

This book is not about Church numbers or how to run the show. It's not about producing a performance to wow those in the pews. Paul said some men plant, others water, but God gives the increase. The Church is not built by any man any more than the universe was created by one.

This book is about challenging the elect in their responsibility to build the Church God's way, by His authority and power, and for His glory. To accomplish the work of building Christ's Church and pleasing Him in the process, a person must understand what Paul meant when he penned these words.

"For consider your calling, brethren, that there were not

many wise according to the flesh, not many mighty, not many noble; but God has chosen the foolish things of the world to shame the wise, and God has chosen the weak things of the world to shame the things which are strong, and the base things of the world and the despised God has chosen, the things that are not, so that He may nullify the things that are, so that no man may boast before God. But by His doing you are in Christ Jesus, who became to us wisdom from God, and righteousness and sanctification, and redemption, so that, just as it is written, "LET HIM WHO BOASTS, BOAST IN THE LORD" (1 Corinthians 1:26-31).

## Thinking Outside the Box

In 2,000 years, many books have been written about the building of Christ's Church. Nevertheless, with many denominations, cults, and Jesus' words warning us to "Beware of the false prophets, who come to you in sheep's clothing..." (Matthew 7:15), what is a person to think?

There are no easy answers or simple ways to know the truth about the Church. The world, the flesh, and the devil are formidable foes who all hate what God is doing through His Church. To discover the truth amid the lies that the devil tells about how God's Church should be built, one must be willing to cast out all preconceived ideas and be willing to accept the admonition of Paul to - "Be not conformed to this world but transformed by the renewing of your mind." (Romans 12:2).

I asked a friend about my first book, The Jesus You Need To Know, "Is it too complicated?" He replied, "It's not too complicated; it's too convicting." If my book about Jesus's life is too convicting, what will people say about the appropriate Biblical way the Church should be built? God's schematic for building His Church will tear at your heart. The real test of your willingness to hear the truth will be to lay down your convictions begotten from false ideas learned from mentors, ministers, and seminary professors who are contrary and oppose God's Word.

Who do you trust, men who may be more mature and godly than yourself or God? Can you think outside the box? There have been times when I gave in to the temptation and accepted the teaching that cost me the truth because of misplaced loyalties. Regaining the truth and taking responsibility for my idolatry has always been excruciating. If you find yourself in such a situation, I pray you do the right thing and honor God.

**The only way to get on the right track is to admit you're going the wrong way.**

# Chapter 1

# I WILL BUILD MY CHURCH
## Authority and Church Building

In Matthew 16:13-19, Jesus declared that He would build His Church. "Now when Jesus came into the district of Caesarea Philippi, He was asking His disciples, "Who do people say that the Son of Man is?" And they said, "Some say John the Baptist; and others, Elijah; but still others, Jeremiah, or one of the prophets." He said to them, "But who do you say that I am?" Simon Peter answered, "You are the Christ, the Son of the living God." And Jesus said to him, "Blessed are you, Simon Barjona, because flesh and blood did not reveal this to you, but My Father who is in heaven. I also say to you that you are Peter, and upon this rock, I will build My Church, and the gates of Hades will not overpower it. I will give you the keys of the kingdom of heaven, and whatever you bind on earth shall have been bound in heaven, and whatever you loose on earth shall have been loosed in heaven."

Peter may have received a key, which represents authority, but chapter sixteen's focus is undeniably upon Jesus Christ as the supreme authority in the Church. Apart from Jesus giving Peter authority, Peter would have no authority, and he only has authority so far as he carries out the desires of Jesus Christ.

Firstly, the authority to build the Church of Jesus Christ comes from the One whose name is Lord. Faith is a critical element of Christianity, and faith is in the Christ of God sent into the world to save men from their sins. The Apostle Paul rightly understood the essential nature of faith in salvation and Church building when he wrote the Book of Romans. Therefore, he tells us quoting from the Old Testament, "THE WORD IS NEAR YOU, IN YOUR MOUTH AND IN YOUR HEART"—that is, the word of faith which we are preaching, that if you confess with your mouth Jesus as Lord, and believe in your heart that God raised Him from the dead, you will be saved; for with the heart a person believes, resulting in righteousness, and with the mouth, he confesses, resulting in salvation." (Romans 10:8-10).

Salvation is revealed through the tongue by confession, beginning in the human heart instead of only in a person's mind. Therefore, it is only authentic when the total man receives it. A study of the New Testament validates the Jewish understanding of the heart, including the mind, the emotions, and the will or the place where people make choices. There can be no Lordship until a person becomes subject to Jesus Christ, like a slave is subject to their master.

The word I refer to in the New Testament in Greek is kurios, which defines the Lord in a Master-slave relationship. For this reason, the writers of the New Testament refer to themselves as slaves of Jesus Christ. Due to the atrocities in human history, the word may be repulsive to some. However, when we speak about the eternal, omnipotent, self-sacrificing God who lovingly sent His Son to die for the sins that otherwise deserve His eternal wrath, we must bow the knee in humble praise and not revolt.

When a person becomes an authentic Christian, they bow their knee to Jesus Christ as Lord. Good Church builders then place all authority at His feet. He is the door to salvation and all authority in leadership. He is the way, and the truth, and the life. Jesus Christ is the source of eternal life because He is the only eternal being. Life originates in no one else. "Every good thing given and every perfect gift is from above, coming down from the Father of lights, with whom there is no variation or shifting shadow." (James 1:17). He is also the only source of good. A Christian can only take credit for his sin and wickedness.

The Church is like everything in the universe; it finds its source in God. God alone, therefore, has the authority. He has the power and holds accountable those who build the Church in His name. Central to Jesus' authority is the truth of His identity as God. Therefore, the question proceeds from Jesus in verse 13, "Who do people say that the Son of Man is?" Jesus underscores the reality that the Church is to be separate from the world by asking first, "Who do people say, or what do people think? Of course, people got it wrong. Some thought that Jesus was John the Baptist raised from the dead, and others one of the prophets, but what was Jesus' reply? He asked Peter, "But who do you say that I am?"

Peter replied, "You are the Christ, the Son of the living God." All are made in God's image and are, therefore, sons of God. However, only one can be said to be the only begotten Son of God because only one is begotten eternally as coming from the God Father, who is also the eternal Son of God.

Therefore, because of Peter's answer, Jesus told him, "Blessed are you, Simon Barjona, because flesh and blood did not reveal this to you, but My Father who is in heaven." Only those related to God in a saving relationship can know the true identity of Jesus Christ in their heart.

Secondly, Jesus said to Peter, "I also say to you that you are Peter, and upon this rock, I will build My Church, and the gates of Hades will not overpower it." Jesus calls Simon by His God-given name, Peter, or a rock. Upon the rock of Peter's profession, Jesus is building His Church. Jesus Christ is the Christ and, thereby, the Son of the living God. Apart from salvation through Jesus Christ, there can be no Church, no people separated from the world to God. It is not built upon an idol, which men follow and curse the true and living God, but upon the living God Himself.

Therefore, when an authentic Christian does not lose track of the reality of Christ's identity and builds according to His revealed will found in His written word, do Jesus' words also apply to him as they did to Peter? "I will give you the keys of the kingdom of heaven, and whatever you bind on earth shall have been bound in heaven, and whatever you loose on earth shall have been loosed in heaven."

We must remember that receiving the keys is never an opportunity to take matters into one's own hands but a responsibility to accomplish God's divine will. That is to say, the builder never builds in his name, for his glory, and according to his desires. Division in the Church confirms that many build in their name because God is neither divided nor confused.

## Jesus' Testimony in Favor of John the Baptist

In chapter eleven of Matthew, we have crucial teaching about Church leadership. "As these disciples of John were going away, Jesus began speaking to the crowds about John:

"What did you go out into the wilderness to see? A reed shaken by the wind? But what did you go out to see? A man dressed in soft clothing? Those who wear soft clothing are in kings' palaces! But what did you go out to see? A prophet? Yes, I tell you, and one who is more than a prophet. This is the one about whom it is written: 'BEHOLD, I AM SENDING MY MESSENGER AHEAD OF YOU, WHO WILL PREPARE YOUR WAY BEFORE YOU.' Truly, I say to you, among those born of women, there has not arisen anyone greater than John the Baptist!" (Matthew 11:7-11).

In Israel's history, at the advent of Christ, four hundred years had passed since a man's voice could be heard declaring the prophecies of God. How is a man to feel when he becomes the voice of Almighty God? The old proverb is power corrupts. Does any person of sound mind deny such reasoning to be reality? One of the reasons that John the Baptist received such high praise from Jesus was his humble Spirit. When the disciples of John began to leave him and follow Jesus and the crowds were no longer coming in great numbers to be baptized by him, he told his disciples.

"A man can receive nothing unless it has been given him from heaven. "You yourselves are my witnesses that I said, 'I am not the Christ,' but, 'I have been sent ahead of Him.' "He who has the bride is the groom, but the friend of the groom, who stands and hears him, rejoices greatly because of the groom's voice. So this joy of mine has been made full. "He must increase, but I must decrease." (John 3:27-30).

John understood well his rightful place. He did not think of himself as standing in Christ's place. "You yourselves are my witnesses that I said, 'I am not the Christ.' Church leaders do well and learn this lesson from John as taught by Jesus. John could have become very inflated about his ministry and calling because there had not been a voice for 400 years. The time was not right until John, but a proud man can give into Satan's temptation, "You are the only one worthy to prophesy." It happens all the time.

Nevertheless, John clearly said, "A man can receive nothing unless it has been given him from heaven." In other words, no man is to lead as one who deserves the honor of leadership, but it must be given from the one who does so according to grace and not works. God created the men he uses and the man who would be the forerunner of Jesus Christ; He made them humble.

At that time, Jesus stated what He thought about the Baptist and how religious leaders criticized Himself and John. Jesus also rebuked the cities of Chorazin and Bethsaida for heaven and earth, that You have hidden these things from the wise and intelligent, and have revealed them to infants. Yes, Father, for this way was well-pleasing in Your sight. All things have been handed over to Me by My Father, and no one knows the Son except the Father; nor does anyone know the Father except the Son, and anyone to whom the Son determines to reveal Him." (Matthew 11:25-27).

In this context, Jesus' teaching should be clear. Intelligence and wisdom obtained by human effort and sinful pride, which James calls demonic, are unacceptable before God. Only people with childlike humility who receive from their heavenly Father what they cannot obtain otherwise are acceptable to God. Apart from divine inspiration, obtained by the working of the Holy Spirit with total dependence upon Him and not human agencies, which he can use but never to replace God the Holy Spirit, there can be no understanding of the truth about Christ or acceptable leadership.

Apart from the ministry of the Holy Spirit, there can be no knowledge of the Father or the Son. The decision to send the Holy Spirit is solely in the desires of the Son of God, and I quote, "...and anyone to whom the Son determines to reveal Him." Jesus does not make determinations built upon human effort and goodness apart from God's saving and sustaining grace.

## The Biblical Testimony of a Hardened Israel

"Nevertheless, with most of them God was not pleased; for their dead bodies were spread out in the wilderness. Now these things happened as examples for us, so that we would not crave evil things as they indeed craved them. Do not be idolaters, as some of them were..." (1 Corinthians 10:5-7).

The warning coming from the Apostle Paul is undeniable. Israel fell in the wilderness; as such, they are to be examples to us and their entire history. During the times of the Judges, as recorded in the book by the same name, the opening chapters tell of the decline in Israel's moral and spiritual life. God continually had to raise judges to save the people from His anger, which otherwise would have been much more severe. The statement that repeats and indicates that their decline was from generation to generation is this one, "But it came about, when the judge died, that they would turn back and act more corruptly than their fathers." (2:19)

The history of Israel is a history of decline. Furthermore, the closing line from the book of Judges tells why. "In those days there was no king in Israel; everyone did what was right in his own eyes." (Judges 21:25). Not having a king was not the problem for Israel; not accepting God as king was their problem. The alternative to God being king is that we make ourselves a king. We wake our own rules by which to live. Furthermore, we set standards by which everyone else is to live while excusing ourselves.

To further complicate this problem of self-rule is generational hardening. From the wanderings of Israel in the wilderness for forty years throughout the 1200 years of their national history, Israel continued to become hardened at heart. Finally, they reached a hardening that sent them into seventy years of exile, followed by 400 years of prophetic silence. When the long-awaited Messiah appeared, the nation was so hard at heart that they called for His death. Even though He vanquished sickness and suffering from their midst and proved Himself to be their Savior, He was not that for which they were looking.

They wanted freedom from the Romans, to live as they pleased and not please God.

## The Message for Today

The Church of Jesus Christ has been in the building for two thousand years. Because Israel's history was recorded partly as an example for us, we should recognize and believe God that we can fall in the same way they did. From 1 Corinthians 10, we should look briefly at the sins noted there but first consider the hardening process.

At Pentecost, revival swept across Jerusalem and Israel, so much so that we can read the Church found favor with all the people. (Acts 2:47). The masses envied Christian love, fellowship, and family life. Eventually, however, the rulers became envious of the Christians and began to stir the hearts of the people against them, which ended in widespread persecution.

In time, revivals like Pentecost always end, and the people, not in total but in part, move into a lifestyle unworthy of the cross of Christ. Error infiltrates the Church, and the hardening of the people's hearts begins to sour a life for Christ. By the fourth century, roles around Christianity started to go the way of Roman Catholicism with a hierarchy of Pope, Cardinals, Bishops, and Priest. Kings and Popes began to battle for power over their countries.

Nine hundred years later, The Reformation started with Martin Luther. Then, Protestants recovered the Gospel, and the true Church was freed from Roman tyranny and began to prosper in the world. Nonetheless, the Church and ministry have not broken free by its captivity to academic achievement, human effort, and an over-emphasis upon the Church as primarily an institution, a hierarchy, and not the Bride of Christ endowed with the very presence of the living God in the person of the Holy Spirit.

Then came the age of the Puritans, who would take the Church to a higher level of holiness but would not reform ministry. Afterward, there were subsequent revivals, such as the Great Awakening, the Second Great Awakening, and the Welsh revivals. The twentieth-century Church left the world in large part worse than before. As a way of life, worldliness supplanted separation from the world, and the Church as a sanctifying force deteriorated. Faith in the God of the Bible and creation was replaced by the unreasonable belief in evolution apart from an intelligent designer.

There are always small revivals in the Church, but a widespread revival worldwide is seldom. In revival, the country is also affected from within by the presence of God in the Church. For the last one hundred years, the only movement in the world has been downward. In conclusion, such has been the plight of Christianity over the past two thousand years.

Let us conclude by considering the sins of Israel mentioned in 1 Corinthians 10 as an example to us. The first was and is Idolatry. For Israel, it was primarily a statue by which men fashioned what they believed to be the image of God. For us, philosophies, higher education, a plethora of possessions, and ease in life go contrary to God's curse upon the serpent, man, woman, and the earth.

Secondly, there is sexual immorality. Although it will never be completely done away, marriage is being systematically eradicated. The warning from God's Holy Word regarding Sodom and Gomorrah has become a great battlefield. Gender roles are also being removed from the arena for all God-given reasons.

In the book of Numbers, testing God comes to a crescendo, and an entire generation is banished from entering the promised land. The vital fact to focus on from Numbers 14 is that the people saw God's works in their deliverance and spurned, rejected them, and chose their sins instead. For two thousand years, the world has rejected the Gospel and replaced it with anti-Christian religions and cultic misrepresentations of Christianity. Large parts of the world are now communist and atheistic. People do not believe in God but in an irrational and unreasoning evolutionary theory. It is assumed that all things, forces, and physical laws came into being without any direction but random and by chance. Insanity has replaced Aristotelian reasoning. Such thinking does not make God happy, and extremely few people care.

Grumbling belongs to all people but is best manifested in nations with abundance, but it is never enough. The people grumble, not knowing what awaits them for all eternity. 1 Corinthians 10:11 concludes this section with the words, "... upon whom the end of the ages has come." For two thousand years, the Church has been in the last days. Peter tells us that a day to the Lord is as a thousand years and a thousand years as a day. I do not know when the Lord will come, but what we know for a fact is what God has said,

"Now we ask you, brothers and sisters, regarding the coming

of our Lord Jesus Christ and our gathering together to Him, that you not be quickly shaken from your composure or be disturbed either by a spirit, or a message, or a letter as if from us to the effect that the day of the Lord has come. No one is to deceive you in any way!" For it will not come unless the apostasy comes first, and the man of lawlessness is revealed, the Son of destruction, who opposes and exalts himself above every so-called God or object of worship, so that he takes his seat in the temple of God, displaying himself as being God." (2 Thessalonians 2:1-4).

We who look expectantly, patiently, and obediently are not to be shaken because the Lord's return and our rapture to Him will not happen until the great falling away occurs first. Yes, the Church will have a great falling away before the Lord returns. Furthermore, the man of lawlessness, anti-Christ, Satan possessing a person will appear first and take his seat in the temple of God, displaying himself as God.

The hardening of the Church will allow these things to take place, but we are not to be shaken because, alive or martyred, we belong to the Lord. We close with a warning from the Apostle Paul. "Do not participate in the useless deeds of darkness, but instead even expose them; for it is disgraceful even to speak of the things which are done by them in secret. But all things become visible when they are exposed by the light, for everything that becomes visible is light. For this reason, it says, "Awake, sleeper, and arise from the dead, and Christ will shine on you." (Ephesians 5:11-14).

"So then, be careful how you walk, not as unwise people but as wise, making the most of your time, because the days are evil. Therefore do not be foolish, but understand what the will of the Lord is. And do not get drunk with wine, in which there is debauchery, but be filled with the Spirit, speaking to one another in psalms and hymns and spiritual songs, singing and making melody with your hearts to the Lord; always giving thanks for all things in the name of our Lord Jesus Christ to our God and Father; and subject yourselves to one another in the fear of Christ." (Ephesians 5:11-21)

# Chapter 2

## ALL AUTHORITY
## The Cosmic Scope of Christ's Authority

It is necessary to start with Christ's authority over his Church. In the final analysis, Christ has sole authority over his Church. However, it is equally important to remember that Christ's authority is not SOLELY over his Church. Indeed, the Great Commission clearly states that "All authority in heaven and on earth has been given" to Christ (Matthew 28:18). This clearly includes the authority over the Church discussed in Chapter 1. Still, all *authority in heaven and earth* implies much more than what people do during worship on a Sunday morning or a Wednesday night.

This dual framing of "heaven and earth" appears to be a reference to the two tables or tablets of the 10 Commandments. The first table, the first five Commandments, deals with your duties to heaven (yes, including that bit about honoring your father and mother). The second table, Commandments Six through Ten, deals with your responsibilities on earth.

A good place to start when contemplating the scope of Christ's authority is with a categorical review of Commandments six through ten. I say categorically because we should understand these commandments as (among other things) the omniscient God claims as the proper way to categorize the world. The modern challenges to the gospel of Christ and the biblical worldview are a challenge at the level of definitional categories. Given that, perhaps it would benefit us to ask, on any given topic, how does the Bible categorize this issue?

## Sixth Commandment

The sixth Commandment, "You shall not murder," is, therefore, a categorical claim by God to authority over man's life. It should be noted that (just as in all of the categories we will discuss) God's declaration of authority over Life is Covenantal. That is to say, there is a relationship with obligations in which God is involved. Therefore, because God is involved, we require His consent to change the relationship in any material fashion.

One of the forgotten truths of the Bible is that life itself is a covenant gift from God. This includes not just your duty to worship and serve him but, in biblical terms, your very breath or, as the word is often translated, "spirit." Again, this is not limited to the initial creation when God put his 'breath' into man (Genesis 2:7), but is a continuing reality; with every breath, you take a distinct covenant gift. (Job 12:10, 27:3, 33:4; Ecclesiastes 12:7;

Acts 17:25). To frame it in the Covenantal terms that the Bible does, we could say that God's side of the Covenant of Life is to keep giving us each breath we need to survive, and the human side is not to violate the image of God.

This is most clearly illustrated in Genesis 6, where God brings what might be called a covenant lawsuit against Mankind for their violence, that is, for their violation of the image of God in other men. "Then God said to Noah, "The end of all flesh has come before Me; for the earth is filled with violence because of them, and behold, I am about to destroy them with the earth." Genesis 6:13. Mankind has breached their side of the Covenant of Life, and therefore, God has the right and, in some sense, the responsibility to stop fulfilling his side of the covenant. God continues: "And behold, I, even I am bringing the flood of water upon the earth, to destroy all flesh in which is the breath of life..." Genesis 6:17. This covenantal nature of this judgment is why He makes a special redemptive covenant with Noah, to preserve not only human life but the lives of all land animals. "But I will establish My Covenant with you; and you shall enter the ark—you and your sons and your wife, and your sons' wives with you. And of every living thing of all flesh, you shall bring two of every kind into the ark, to keep them alive with you; they shall be male and female." Genesis 6:18-19.

One of the reasons we may not be very familiar with the covenantal nature of life is that, throughout the pattern of redemptive history, God continues to layer on additional redemptive covenants. Particularly in his dealings with Israel, He tends to base the later judgments on those particular covenants instead of the underlying Covenant of Life. But God still does use this language, mainly when dealing with a pagan king. *"...You have exalted yourself against the Lord of heaven;...and you have praised the gods of silver and gold, of bronze, iron, wood and stone, which do not see, hear or understand. But the God in whose hand are your life-breath and all your ways, you have not glorified."* Daniel 5:23.

This covenant is the ancient origin of the taboo against genocide. Wanton killing, particularly of innocents, has been feared for explicitly religious reasons since recorded history began by men who had no earthly reason to fear killing their enemies. And when killings, particularly of children, were done, it was done skulking in the dark, with all involved sworn to secrecy on whatever dark gods they worshiped. We should tremble to know the bloodguilt of the industrial-grade American abortion mills will, before 2050 at the current rates, eclipse the number of innocent lives taken in all the bloody tyranny of 20th Century Soviet Russia and Maoist China combined.

The spiritual covenant of life requires us to have only one God before Him, the author and source of all life. This covenantal nature of life is the inescapable testimony of the Bible and the fundamental ground for our duty to God as God. And as a reminder, this is the only application of this principle to our duty on earth.

# Seventh Commandment

Continuing with our discussion of the scope of the authority given to Christ is the Seventh Commandment "You shall not commit adultery." As a categorical matter, a claim of sovereignty over all sexual behavior is what defines a valid and ideal marriage. This goes far beyond the simple definition of marriage between one man and one woman for life (though it CERTAINLY includes it).

I should note that these categories are implicit in the sacred duty imposed in the words of this command. Embedded in the word for adultery is the idea of the husband and wife, the vow of fidelity, and, properly understood, the life-long union. The command is meaningless if any of these conceptual categories need to be redefined and reinterpreted.

Modern American Christian teaching still affirms the covenant status of marriage, that it is sacred and is a covenant. However, most Christians today think of this mainly as a New Testament feature due to the solid bridal language in Ephesians 5 and Revelation 21. This is likely because God frequently uses marriage as a metaphor for his relationship with his covenant people. But in fact, the analogy goes back to Exodus, with what scholars generally recognize as a betrothal oath in Exodus 19:4-6. We also see God prosecuting a covenantal lawsuit for the violations of this marital covenant in Ezekiel, Hosea, and Isaiah.

But God is also involved in natural physical marriages on a

profound level. Jesus says marriage is a life-long bond because of the nature of the creation categories of male and female. Further, he notes that it is God himself who joins the married couple together. (Matthew 19:6; Mark 10:9). God is involved in the marriage covenant; therefore, the man and woman need to get His permission to make any material changes in the arrangement between them.

# Eighth Commandment

As Pierre Viret, the "angel of the reformation," wrote in his wonderful short book, "Thou Shalt Not Steal," the eighth Commandment is fundamental to our understanding of what we might call "core economics" or "value-creation." Just as with the Seventh Commandment, for this Commandment to have any meaning, we must apply the ancient understanding of property rights. I do not say "private" property because, in our current culture, private property has become synonymous with individual property.

This emphasis on individual property has led to some of our current issues, where we pretend that specific collective organizations (companies) are 'persons' to allow them to hold property. We pretend that other collectives (governments), not being 'persons,' are somehow immune to the dictates of the Eighth Commandment. The Biblical approach is to apply a much broader notion of property rights, which can be held by individuals, tribes, or other collective groups and certainly apply to the government. See 1 Kings 21.

In context, the Commandment not to steal also includes duties to one's ancestors and one's house, who would leave property to you on certain conditions. The most common condition was that you continued to maintain the name and honor of your household and that you did not sell your inheritance, usually lands with an attached business. The story of Naboth's vineyard is an excellent example. "But Naboth said to Ahab, "May the Lord keep me from giving you what I have received from my fathers." 1 Kings 21:3. Naboth refuses to obey the king when he has every incentive to do so because that would be stealing from his ancestors and ultimately from God. It is Naboth's obedience to the category of the Eighth Commandment that motivates him here.

This requirement not to steal applies to tangible pieces of property but also includes relational obligations to provide and even to take people into one's home. This drives the ritual transaction in the book of Ruth, where Boaz buys the right to marry Ruth. The field was not just a piece of property; it was also (likely) an estate with a house and, in this case, a wife who would need to be married.

Interestingly, in this context, the word economics (Oikosnomos) originally meant household law or the principles governing a household for profit creation. In the New Testament, Paul instructs everyone, including slaves, to seek the good of the household to which they belonged, as though they were working for the Lord. There is an understanding that God is involved in labor and capital, finance and real property, technology and art, and all the attendant rights and responsibilities.

For our purposes, this Commandment is an explicit claim of authority by the Lord Jesus Christ over everything from high finance to your house design and who has the right to live with you there. No portion of a person's economic life, whether acting as an individual or for any form of collective organization, is beyond the scope of God's law, and the biblical Commandment is not to steal.

# Ninth Commandment

The Ninth Commandment specifically refers to public testimony, likely in a judicial setting. The literal meaning of the Commandment is to make it a crime to falsely accuse your neighbor of a crime or provide false evidence used to convict such a person. But just as adultery is the pinnacle of a whole litany of sexual sins, the Ninth Commandment is the vile culmination of a host of untruths and falsehoods of varying types.

I will mention that the Ninth Commandment, the commitment to truth in public discourse, is in some ways still greatly revered and protected under the United States system. The free speech protections in the First Amendment to the United States Constitution are directly drawn from the

Protestant understanding of what was required under the Ninth Commandment. This is why, as we fully and finally depart from the heritage of cultural Christianity in the United States (for better and for worse, primarily for worse), those legal protections are being eroded, vilified, and ultimately revoked.

On the other hand, the respect for truth in our public discourse, more generally, has been eroded to the point where people lie with impunity while campaigning for political office and where there is absolutely no trust between political parties. Another way of putting this is that obedience to the Ninth Commandment is essential to maintain a republican (that is, a representative) form of government.

Legislatures or Assemblies, broadly stated, are entities where the group's decisions are not dictated from above but discerned by more extensive and smaller groups, with mutual debate, checks and balances, and the assorted safeguards accompanying a realization that no one is free from the corruption of sin. Specifically, the virtue of truth-telling, of sacred spaces where no false word can be uttered, is the core requirement of a functioning legislature. Legislative types of institutions depend on mutual faith in the truth-telling of both parties to allow the debate to move forward. To put it another way, you CAN NOT debate with someone unless they have the exact source of authority that you do and they are willing to engage with you truthfully. This is particularly important to Christians, given that the literal meaning of Ekklesia, the word translated as Church in the Bible, is Legislative Assembly.

Perhaps, for this reason, it is still understood in conservative Evangelical circles that speaking the truth matters in every area of our life. Once upon a time, it was the first of our core values as Americans ("truth, justice, and the American way." The Ninth Commandment makes clear that truth always matters in the calculus of God. That conservative understanding that to build anything other than a tyrannical hierarchy, you must speak the truth IS a covenantal understanding, albeit an unconscious one.

# Tenth Commandment

The Tenth and final Commandment is in and of itself a microcosm of the five-fold pattern. Many focus on the house, the wife, household servants, herds, or "anything that belongs to your neighbor." The secret of the Tenth Commandment is not in all of the specific variations of the prohibition on covetousness. It is the relationship with the neighbor that is being protected.

The categorical understanding here answers the question, "who is my neighbor." As Christians, we can 'flip to the back of the book' and answer the Samaritan is my neighbor. In fact, we might observe that in the ancient Near East culture, if you refrained from coveting just the first four things explicitly listed, you would genuinely be "loving your neighbor as yourself."

But it's critically important to recognize that Jesus was NOT TEACHING SOMETHING NEW in that parable. He was simply explicating something that the 'teachers of Israel' should have already seen from the text. The 10th Commandment, by defining our duties negatively to our neighbor, tells us some critical things about the divine categories of neighbor.

The word neighbor or fellow citizen means everyone who owes loyalty to the same sovereign (literally, in the flock of the same shepherd). In a Christian sense, this includes everyone because everyone owes allegiance to God as sovereign. This is not to say that they HAVE loyalty to the rightful king, but that they owe it.

The 10th Commandment indicates that while it might be acceptable (indeed even praiseworthy) to compete for honor or prestige, your interactions with others should be characterized by a desire for a win-win. Both you and the other party grow stronger, or at a minimum, not a desire to harm or weaken others. The emphasis is on seeking the common good or the commonwealth.

To the degree that a political system becomes used to satisfy the covetousness of some person or group, that system is broken. By the same token, if the covetousness of the persons wielding power can be restricted, almost any political system can function reasonably well. Just as truth is the essential ingredient for a good legislative process, opposing covetousness is a core ingredient of the political process, or what we might call good governance.

Another way of understanding the 10th Commandment is from the perspective of monopoly. God's law gives exclusive rights to specific people over specific things and relationships. For example, a husband and wife have exclusive rights over one another's bodies. In the tribal structure of ancient Israel, the house was associated with hereditary lands (Numbers 36), religious duties (Leviticus 17:27-29, Numbers 18), and even governmental offices (1 Chronicles 8, 17). Challenging these monopolies, these exclusive rights, was not merely an affront to the rights holders but to God as the sovereign grantor of the exclusive rights in question.

From the perspective of our categorical analysis, this is an unambiguous claim of authority in every aspect of governmental policy. We live in a day and age where much of our political decisions revolve around not 'if' we will be covetous but which group's covetousness will win the day. Further, the corruption of our political offices for personal financial gain and the newfound ability of state and local governments to shut businesses down in a shockingly arbitrary fashion is clear evidence that we have not kept the 10th Commandment.

## Conclusion

In conclusion, the authority of Christ, as proclaimed by the Bible, extends to every area of life: The spiritual, sexual, political, governmental, and everything in between, even (and perhaps especially) economics. This initial insight implies another, which is that the Bible provides instruction for MULTIPLE authority structures, which are different and governed by different rules. We should be careful, therefore, not to assume that simply because the Bible describes an authority structure and gives instruction for how that structure can operate righteously, such a structure can be implemented wholesale in the Church.

The most significant danger (and one which the Bible explicitly addresses) is the danger of the Priest-King. We are kings and priests, but the Bible clearly discusses the risks of merging political power with religious authority. Unfortunately, we find ourselves in a position today where the overwhelming majority of our churches have adopted a monarchic or monopolistic-style organization, which, while powerful and righteous in its own sphere (as a 10th Commandment structure), is inappropriate and the cause of much wickedness in the Church.

# Chapter 3

# DEATH WILL NOT PREVAIL
## The Fear of God and Church Building

In the previous chapter, Greg stepped up the game by focusing our attention on the applicability of the Bible to all aspects of life, including what we call secular institutions. Of course, the Bible is relevant to the Church, but it is equally essential in government, marriage, and the conscience of all people.

Sinners design their best lives for the descendants of Adam's rebellious race; God is not part of the process. For this reason, most religious groups manufacture religion to fit their beliefs.

The Old Testament is the history of God's favored people, Israel, selected by God's grace and not their goodness. Like Elijah on Mount Carmel, Jesus, God incarnate, spoke against prophets, and as Savior, God's fire fell on Him at Calvary's cross.

Syncretism is the merging of different religions, misunderstanding that all religions do not worship the one true and living God. That is why God's word, the Bible, rejects and declares false prophets. "But false prophets also arose among the people, just as there will also be false teachers among you, who will secretly introduce destructive heresies, even denying the Master who bought them, bringing swift destruction upon themselves." (2 Peter 2:1)

False religion within sinful men is self-absorbed and, therefore, out of touch with reality, enabling us to live without a genuine fear of God.

## Sinful Men Lack the Fear of God

The Bible is sixty-six books of self-revelation by God. He reveals Himself on the pages of scripture as the creator of all things. Furthermore, God is eternal, outside of time, without beginning or end. God is three persons in one God. He is all-knowing, everywhere present, and all-powerful. God is infinite and perfect; He has relationships to perfection within the Trinity and, therefore, needs nothing.

Furthermore, creation adds nothing to God. Therefore, man owes his existence entirely to God's unbenefited beneficence. What has God received for the gift of life from all those created in His image? They prove their hatred for His revealed will by torturing and killing those who've repented of sin and believed in him.

"THERE IS NO FEAR OF GOD BEFORE THEIR EYES." concludes a nine-verse litany of evils in the heart of men devoted to sin and supreme wretchedness. In a world full of selfish hatred, men judge one another by standards they set for others while excusing themselves of everything they can. In this same world are erected courts of law, judges who pass sentences, prisons for guilty men, and police meant to bring men to justice.

Furthermore, with the law on the books, some judges are often paid off, some police do evil alongside the guilty, and the prisons breed worse criminals. The scriptures do not say in vain, "THERE IS NO FEAR OF GOD BEFORE THEIR EYES." how, in the name of everything good, could men behave in such a vile way and have a fear of God?

## A Biblical Fear of God

There is nothing less terrifying than facing a foe you know you can't possibly beat but who also possesses an indomitable resolve to destroy you. Certain people, for whatever reasons, have no tinge of remorse for killing someone. That is the kind of person to fear.

However, God does not think or feel from such an uncaring state. God is the source of all good, and righteousness, holiness, and purity come from Him. Such things are not outside of Him but find their origin in Him.

On the other side of God is the hatred of all that is evil. God brought the Jewish people through the Red Sea and eventually established them in Canaan's land, which became the nation of Israel. During Israel's history, God brought judgments and many warnings through the prophets about their impending doom. Sinful people do not listen or take appropriate actions to avoid destruction.

In Jeremiah, God declared His holiness and Israel's waywardness. "Because they have filled this place with the blood of the innocent and have built the high places of Baal to burn their sons in the fire as burnt offerings to Baal, a thing which I never commanded or spoke of, nor did it ever enter My mind;" (Jeremiah 19:4, 5, 7) The innocent blood referred to was the sacrifice of babies to appease their false gods.

God knows all things; He knows the end from the beginning. So when He says, "...not did it ever enter my mind..." He means the idea did not find its source in Him. Holiness comes from God; all evil originates in men and fallen angels.

Anyone who does not get angry at evil and injustice is evil and unjust. It is a horrible thing to declare God as cruel and unfair. In the nineteenth century, a great evil began to arise; so-called scholars of the Bible started to erase all thoughts of an angry God and declared Him to be only a God of love. Such men had no fear of God before their eyes; even worse, they seduced others to further depths of fearlessness before God.

Such teachings existed as early as the second century but have become widely accepted today. With all its unbiblical dogma, Roman Catholicism taught hellfire for nine hundred years. The Protestant Church also taught the inescapable truths from scripture of God's holy wrath at the Reformation. People can change the words of the Bible if they like, but only a person without the fear of God would dare to do so.

## A Criminal's Fear of God

Searching the web as part of my preparation for this chapter, I found a plethora of articles devoted to eradicating a Biblical fear of God. Often, people do not realize that God is one. Therefore, the God who inspired the writing of the New Testament equally inspired the Old. A low view of God is the cause of many deceptions. God does not change, and He does not make mistakes.

Those who criticize Biblical teaching must think themselves more knowledgeable than those inspired by God. As the wise man Solomon stated, "For in many dreams and many words there is emptiness. Rather, fear God." - Solomon (Ecclesiastes. 5:7)

"The fear of the LORD is the beginning of wisdom" (Psalm 111:10). A criminal started his journey to fearing the LORD and wisdom at the cross. At Christ's crucifixion, they also nailed two criminals; both hurled abuses at Him once upon the cross. However, one was changed, received Jesus as Lord, and began rebuking the other criminal. "Do you not even fear God, since you are under the same sentence of condemnation?" (Luke 23:4)

When the converted criminal saw Jesus as God, he feared. What words! "Do you not even fear God..." Where was God?

He was hanging right beside him. Two men were paying a death sentence, and both began abusing Jesus, according to Mark 15:32. They wanted freedom from the penalty for their evil deeds. Upon repentance, the one criminal recognized his evil soul, therefore, proclaimed, "...you are under the same sentence of condemnation..." First, an earthly court condemned him, then his conscience, prompted by the Holy Spirit. Of whom Jesus spoke, "And He, when He comes, will convict the world concerning sin and righteousness and judgment;" (John 16:8)

There is no doubt about the transformation of the criminal's thoughts and convictions, which are never more sincere than at the point of death. "And we indeed are suffering justly, for we are receiving what we deserve for our deeds..." (Vs. 41). He was guilty and knew it for the first time to the point of repentance. What changed his mind and heart was an honest view of God. "...but this man has done nothing wrong." There was one sinless man in all human history, and this criminal realized it by the grace of God.

Kings have ruled on God's behalf, but only God is the authentic ruler of His kingdom. Hence, the criminal's words, "Jesus, remember me when You come into Your kingdom!" The kingdom of God is the kingdom belonging to Jesus. He created all things, He is before all things, and all things owe complete allegiance to Him and Him alone. Loyalty began with fear for this criminal and must start with fear for all sinful people. Our devotion must begin with trepidation, also.

# Biblical and UnBiblical Fear

Jesus said, "Do not fear those who kill the body but are unable to kill the soul, but rather fear Him who can destroy both soul and body in hell." (Matthew 10:28). The most natural reaction to pain and death is fear. We all have experienced it to one extent or another. Jesus contrasts two sources of death; He is not telling us to avoid the unavoidable but to avoid the fear of men.

Solomon tells us, "The fear of man brings a snare, but he who trusts in the LORD will be exalted." (Proverbs 29:25). The fear of man brings unbelief in God. Thus, Solomon contrasted a trap with being exalted. The temptation is to fear men or trust in the Lord. Those who walk by faith will be exalted because they exalt the Lord by trusting Him.

We must trust the Lord and not fear those who can kill the body. First, we must understand that Jesus said the fear of death would not overpower the Church. That is a statement of fact from the One who has all authority and power to keep His word. After asking Peter, "who do you say that I am?" He received the answer that He was Christ, the Son of the living God. Therefore, upon the rock of Peter's profession of faith in Christ, Jesus said. "I will build My church, and the gates of Hades will not overpower it" (Matthew 16:15-18).

God's power is unleashed when a person's faith becomes a fact in their heart. When the thief on the cross accepted the reality that he was guilty and condemned by Roman law, he placed his faith in Christ and was forgiven and freed from the law of God. That moment in time is the most graphic illustration of saving faith. For the thief to see his salvation, he needed to turn his head. Then he could behold the face of God and know he was loved and forgiven.

## Overcoming the Gates of Hell

When facing death, we look to the One who has all authority over it, the Lord Jesus Christ. When looking to God or Christ, we need to know what we are looking at, best described by His name. One of God's complex names is in Psalm 20, Yehovah Nissi or the LORD (I AM) your banner. "May we shout for joy at your victory and raise a banner in the name of our God" (Psalm 20:5).

When the Psalmist says, "...we shout for joy at your victory..." he speaks of the victory the Lord Jesus secured for His people. In Old Testament days, a banner was generally a pole upon which shiny objects were attached, making it better to observe, much like the flag we fly today. The flag symbolizes what we fight for and the person we trust to win us victory. The military relies on its leaders and, ultimately, their king.

In Christianity, our God and King died for us to have victory. Therefore, Psalm 20 tells us. "Now I know that the LORD sees His anointed; He answers him from His holy heaven with the saving power of His right hand" (Psalm 20:50). Christ is the anointed Son that God sees, and He is also the saving power of His right hand. Jesus is always seated at the right hand of God the Father.

"We will sing for joy over your victory, and in the name of our God, we will set up our banners." The Christian's banner is the cross of Christ because Christ won the victory upon it. Therefore, joy over God's victory is in Christ.

Many martyrs have been victorious in the face of death. They held the glory of Christ's death in their heart during the moment of their death and entered into His victory. It was the Apostle Paul who declared his victory in Christ. "I count all things to be loss in view of the surpassing value of knowing Christ Jesus my Lord, for whom I have suffered the loss of all things, and count them but rubbish so that ... I may know Him and the power of His resurrection and the fellowship of His sufferings, being conformed to His death" (Philippians 3:8, 10)

The Christian has assured victory by seeing Jesus. "Therefore, since the children share in flesh and blood, He likewise also partook of the same, that through death He might render powerless him who had the power of death, that is, the devil, and might free those who through fear of death were subject to slavery all their lives" (Hebrews 2:14, 15). God secured victory over death by becoming a man and rendering the devil's words powerless. The believer's death is a victory because it does not end in a grave but in the presence of the Lord.

It is not as though believers never experience the temptation to fear death and suffering or that they do not hear lies from the devil to do so. However, ultimately, they have the source of victory - Christ. "For since He Himself was tempted in that which He has suffered, He is able to come to the aid of those who are tempted." (Hebrews 2:18).

## Living Out a Biblical Death

The followers of Jesus Christ are to face death. "I say to you, My friends, do not be afraid of those who kill the body and after that have no more that they can do. But I will warn you whom to fear: fear the One who, after He has killed, has authority to cast into hell; yes, I tell you, fear Him!" (Luke 12:4, 5)

Regardless of what the evolutionist propagates, the grave has no final say. There is a heaven, and there is a hell. For six thousand years, men have chosen how to live for themselves or upon repentance and faith in God. To live for God, a man must die to his selfish desires, will, and purposes. Those who overcome the temptation to exalt themselves over God are promised a crown of life. "Blessed is a man who perseveres under trial; for once he has been approved, he will receive the crown of life which the Lord has promised to those who love Him" (James 1:12; emphasis added). The choice is not merely a matter of our will; it is whether or not we love God because the promise is to those who love God.

God's promised crown is called a crown of life, which He

offered the Church in Smyrna. "Do not fear what you are about to suffer. Behold, the devil is about to cast some of you into prison, that you may be tested, and you will have tribulation ten days. Be faithful until death, and I will give you the crown of life" Revelation 2:10.

In God's economy, death to self by overcoming sin's temptation is synonymous with faithfulness unto death. The temptation in prison is to abandon one's conviction and abdicate allegiance to Jesus Christ. Christ tells Christians not to quit their confidence in Him. He never stopped, though. He faced the fires of hell for everyone for whom He died.

Who do you love - the world or God? Where are your convictions? There are many promises in God's word concerning believers and non-believers; which are you? Some men will not trust in what God promised in the next life. "See the man who would not make God his refuge, but trusted in the abundance of his riches and sought refuge in his own destruction!" (Psalm 52:7). Saved men wait for God and do not desire their best life now. "The LORD favors those who fear Him, those who wait for His lovingkindness" (Psalm 147:11).

Upon the conviction of such men, God builds His Church.

# Chapter 4

# A Citizen of No Ordinary City
## The Christian Purpose of Liberty

Paul answered, "I am a Jew, from Tarsus in Cilicia, a citizen of no ordinary city. Please let me speak to the people." Acts 21:39

## The Mandate of our Christian Identity

As we look at the mandate of our Christian identity throughout the New Testament, one of the themes that quickly becomes clear is our calling to a kind of martial vigor, a soldier's calling, if you will, while simultaneously being a sojourner in our daily experience.

Christian identity may make better sense if we put it into a story with whom every person who traveled in the First Century (as Paul did) would have been intimately familiar. Let me set the scene.

You are a citizen of Rome on a journey. Maybe you are traveling on a ship. Perhaps you are part of a caravan to faraway

India or, even further, China. Maybe you are one of several Roman officers on a detachment far out on the frontier (say in a little border town called Londinium). And then something happens. A war starts, the trade roads close, and the shipwrecks.

You are going to miss the time. You are a stranger and sojourner, perhaps forever. You may never see the city whose citizenship you bear so proudly ever again. What do you do?

To answer that, let us take a step back. In the Roman view, a citizen was physically, mentally, and morally fit to serve and protect the glory of their city. The most basic form of such service was vital, to defend your town in her distress, like the men on the walls of Helm's Deep in The Two Towers movie. If you were unfit for such service, physically couldn't hold a sword, and lacked the mental capacity to follow orders effectively, most importantly, if you were a coward and therefore morally defective, you could lose your citizenship and even face treason charges. You were also unfit if your citizenship itself, by ascension or birth, and your obligation to show up on the wall and defend your city in her hour of need. Then it was not permissible to consider whether your city would succeed in her struggle.

But there was a subtler understanding, particularly around the time of the First Century. See, Rome was well into her military phase by this point. Many Roman citizens, perhaps even a majority, would live and die without ever seeing the physical walls of the city itself. Further, the Pax Romana was in full swing, and it was almost unthinkable that an enemy would ever threaten the physical walls of Rome. You might have isolated incidents of rebellion or the odd coup attempt. Violence akin to what we might call terrorism was also possible. But, in general, Romans felt about the Roman heartland the way Americans thought about the continental United States—no mainstream American worries about a foreign army conquering Kansas. Let's see a feel-good movie about the heartland getting invaded, but in actual geopolitical calculations.

So then, what did the citizenship of all these people who had never seen Rome's walls mean? By the time of Christ, the answer was well established; it meant loyalty and devotion to Rome's laws, customs, and culture. It meant creating and maintaining a culture that would produce Roman citizens who would carry on the Roman way and advance the glory of that way, regardless of whether they ever saw or would ever see the actual city itself.

Beloved, I urge you as sojourners and exiles to abstain from the passions of the flesh, which wage war against your soul. Keep your conduct among the Gentiles honorable so that when they speak against you as evildoers, they may see your good deeds and glorify God on the day of visitation.

## The Positive Duty of our Christian Identity

As shown in 1 Peter 2:13-14, this was a positive duty. It was not enough to merely avoid harming the interests of your city. Rather, the expectation was that the trajectory of your life, including your career or business, would advance the interests and adorn the city's glory. No matter where you found yourself, it was your responsibility to 1. Figure out how to advance your city as best as possible, and 2. SPEND THE REST OF YOUR LIFE DOING IT.

At a minimum, this duty included raising your children to be Romans. To be devoted in this same way to the city. It included raising sons and daughters who viewed the laws, the customs, and the honor of Rome as paramount. This duty is why the citizenship statement in Ephesians 2 leads seamlessly (in the Roman mind) into the "household code" of Ephesians 4-6, which deals explicitly with the duties of husbands and wives, fathers and children, etc. These extended families or households were little enclaves of the city from which they sprang. That citizenship included those born or adopted into the family despite being in a foreign land.

"So then you are no longer strangers and aliens, but you are fellow citizens with the saints and members of the household of God..." Ephesians 2:19

## Rejecting a Foreign Identity

If a group of Roman citizens was cut off in a foreign land, say in China or India, the local potentates came to them and said, "We are fine with you living here. We will even give you land and make you nobles. But you have to recognize that this is our land, with our laws and our customs, and our practices. If you are going to be here, you have to abandon your Roman citizenship and your Roman nature." Any citizen of Rome, from a gray-haired elder all the way down to a teenage schoolboy, would instinctively reject such a demand.

The Christian counterpart to this is Philippians 3. In describing those who turn against the Gospel, Paul gives us this contrast:

'For many, of whom I have often told you and now tell you even with tears, walk as enemies of the cross of Christ. Their end is destruction, their god is their belly, and they glory in their shame, with minds set on earthly things. But our citizenship is in heaven, and from it, we await a Savior, the Lord Jesus Christ, who will transform our lowly body to be like his glorious body, by the power that enables him even to subject all things to himself." Philippians 3:19-21

## Building an Enclave to Reflect
## Our Christian Identity

So when citizens of a Greco-roman city found themselves shipwrecked on the African Coast, stranded in the middle of India or China, or far out in the backwater frontier of Britain, they knew what to do. They would build an enclave, a space, a micro-city that reflected the specific character of the city from which they sprang. They would create spaces where their distinctive city's customs, laws, and culture could operate and be passed on.

They would, in the words of Hebrews 11, "Look forward to the city with eternal foundations, whose designer and builder is God."

If you can't get back to your city, you build a piece of your city where you are. I have twice now mentioned London, which is the remarkable success story of this view of the rights and duties of a citizen. As with any actual historical civilization, there are a million ways of telling the story of the British Empire, but the most interesting is to say it is the story of a group of citizens who never stopped building their city. Now, the name and language changed, and to some extent, the customs were quite different by the time the British Empire rose. But they saw themselves, quite self-consciously, as the true heirs and worthy successors of the Roman Empire.

Think about that. A group of citizens so committed to the ideals and virtues of their city that they didn't give up, even when the actual, physical earthly town fell. Rome's power faded, and eventually, the city itself fell, never to regain its military strength or world-dominating control.

But the Roman citizens posted in Londinium, their children, and their children's children down through the ages never quit. And it is that character, commitment, and the fundamental belief Paul invokes when he uses the word Citizen.

We are strangers and aliens in this world. We are shipwrecked.

In human terms, it cut off from much of the military might and political power of the city (though not as much as you might think). But we are capable and, more importantly, commanded to live and die as Citizens of a heavenly city.

The Citizens of Rome and the men of the British Empire were willing to lay down their lives rather than betray their love for their city. How can we do less when we look forward to having such a better city?

"But you have come to Mount Zion and the city of the living God, the heavenly Jerusalem, and to innumerable angels in festal gathering, and to the assembly of the firstborn who are enrolled in heaven, and to God, the judge of all, and to the spirits of the righteous made perfect, and to Jesus, the mediator of a new covenant, and to the sprinkled blood that speaks a better word than the blood of Abel." Hebrew 12:22-24

# Chapter 5

## SHEPHERDS IN CHURCH BUILDING
### Humble Sheep Become Faithful Shepherds

It is well known that sheep are some of the most needy animals. They can't sufficiently clean themselves, and they can die from their uncleanness. Sheep have no natural defenses, which makes them easy prey for predators. The creator God made sheep to use them as an example of sinful people. The Icelandic leadersheep is a sheep breed selected and known for its particular behavioral traits, such as leading the flock and bringing it home from pasture in case of danger. Those traits are also said to be beneficial in areas with high predator pressure. What is equally valid is that sheep follow mindlessly, whether it is a shepherd or a leadersheep, so if the leader goes off a cliff, so goes the flock.

"When Jesus went ashore, He saw a large crowd, and He felt compassion for them because they were like sheep without a shepherd; and He began to teach them many things." Mark 6:34

# Israel's Illuminating Sunlight

The large crowd for whom Jesus felt compassion were Israelites. They were the most fastidious, meticulous followers of any religion of their time. Furthermore, the religion they followed was given to them by the one true and living God, as evidenced by the Red Sea crossing and the destruction of Egypt, to whom they were slaves.

The law they followed was given to Moses on Mount Sinai. It included the creation account, the fall into sin in the Garden of Eden, the reign of death in chapter five (which revealed death as a consequence of sin), and the violence that ensued for fourteen hundred years, leading to the worldwide flood. During Israel's forty-year wandering in the desert due to their disobedience and unbelief toward God, four other books were written, including all the law details and the first of two covenants between God and His people. Furthermore, in all thirty-nine books, Israel's history of their sins was recorded, as well as five wisdom books and the prophets who announced the people's evil ways and the promises of their eventual restoration by God's grace.

Compared to all previous generations, nations, and people groups

Israel became privy to more information about humanity and God than any other. Furthermore, alongside the moral law in the first five books, known as the Torah, is the law of ordinances to be carried out by the priesthood, which all typified the coming of the Messiah for the salvation of God's people.

Knowing the privileges given to Israel by God's grace, why did Jesus feel compassion for the crowd as sheep not having a shepherd?

## Israel's Miraculous Beginning and Apostasy

With a miraculous hand, God brought Israel from slavery to a land flowing with milk and honey. From the beginning and throughout their history, God's point is that the people were never worthy of His saving hand. Moses turned a staff into a snake and the Nile into a river of blood. Ten plagues by God destroyed Egypt for Pharaoh to let the people go. At the last, Pharoah relented, but still, he chased Israel in the desert to the destruction of his army. However, was the response by the children of Israel any different?

As God responded to Pharaoh, He also did to Israel during their forty-year wandering, as found in Numbers 14:19-23. God would have destroyed them without Moses' intercession for the people. "Pardon, I pray, the iniquity of this people according to the greatness of Your lovingkindness, just as You also have forgiven this people, from Egypt even until now." So the LORD said, "I have pardoned them according to your word; but indeed, as I live, all the earth will be filled with the glory of the LORD. "Surely all the men who have seen My glory and My signs which I performed in Egypt and in the wilderness, yet have put Me to the test these ten times and have not listened to My voice, shall by no means see the land which I swore to their fathers, nor shall any of those who spurned Me see it."

Of the entire generation that entered the promised land, only two and the second generation got to enter, but none from the first. Verses twenty-eight through thirty-four give God's further response. "Say to them, 'As I live,' says the LORD, 'just as you have spoken in My hearing, so I will surely do to you; your corpses will fall in this wilderness, even all your numbered men, according to your complete number from twenty years old and upward, who have grumbled against Me. 'Surely, you "not come into the land where I swore to settle you, except Caleb, the son of Jephunneh, and Joshua, the son of Nun. 'Your children, however, whom you said would become a prey—I will bring them in, and they will know the land which you have rejected. 'But as for you, your corpses will fall in this wilderness. 'Your sons shall be shepherds for forty years in the wilderness, and they will suffer for your unfaithfulness, until your corpses lie in the wilderness. 'According to the number of days which you spied out the land, forty days, for every day you shall bear your guilt a year, even forty years, and you will know My opposition."

An entire generation was lost in the wilderness due to God's standards. Verse 24 gives us the standard. "But My servant Caleb, because he has had a different spirit and has followed Me fully, I will bring into the land which he entered, and his descendants shall take possession of it." The Old Testament included that if a person is to inherit eternal life, he must be born again (John

3, Jesus' conversation with Nicodemus). This truth may be hard to accept, considering the prolific teaching of the Holy Spirit only for the Church. Still, such education notwithstanding, the Bible teaches something else, Numbers 27:18. "So the LORD said to Moses, "Take Joshua the son of Nun, a man in whom is the Spirit, and lay your hand on him."

Israel's deliverance from their slavery in Egypt was a miraculous act of God's grace, but it was not without God's justice upon an evil and unconverted people. When the writer to the Hebrews recounted the forty-year wanding to warn the Church, he said the following in Hebrews 3:12-19.

## The New Testament Writer to the Hebrews Warned of Apostasy

"Take care, brethren, that there not be in any one of you an evil, unbelieving heart that falls away from the living God. But encourage one another day after day, as long as it is still called "Today," so that none of you will be hardened by the deceitfulness of sin. For we have become partakers of Christ, if we hold fast the beginning of our assurance firm until the end, while it is said, "Today if you hear His voice, do not harden your hearts, as when they provoked Me," For who provoked Him when they had heard? Indeed, did not all those who came out of Egypt led by Moses? And with whom was He angry for forty years? Was it not with those who sinned, whose bodies fell in the wilderness?

And to whom did He swear that they would not enter His rest, but to those who were disobedient? So we see that they were not able to enter because of unbelief."

Faith, as said so frequently today, is the key to salvation. However, the nature of faith is equally important. Faith must have a transformative element attached to it if it is to be saving faith. Faith is not a get-out-of-jail-free card. If faith is cheap, it causes the same reaction of anger, resentment, and justice from God as Israel's flight from Egypt. God is the same yesterday, today, and forever.

## Moses Warned Israel of Apostasy

Apostasy is to fall away from the faith. Some get confused about falling away as if someone is losing their salvation. Not at all! Persevering faith saves because it enables the person to believe to the end, including martyrdom, separation from the evil world system, and all forms of idolatry. Unbelief, masquerading as saving faith, always causes a person to fall away, whether they leave the Church or not. Therefore, Moses instructed and warned the people about the covenant God was making with Israel beginning in Deuteronomy 29:18.

"So that there will not be among you a man or woman, or family or tribe, whose heart turns away today from the LORD our God, to go and serve the gods of those nations; that there will not be among you a root bearing poisonous fruit and wormwood." To turn away is to apostate. Such a person turns away from God and toward the idols of the nations. Again, such a person never possessed the faith that saves but a mere intellectual understanding of God and His ways. The person never embraced the truth of saving grace wholeheartedly by mind, emotions, and will or the places they make the choices that matter before God.

The apostate's heart is examined and defined by the words of Moses in verse nineteen. "It shall be when he hears the words of this curse that he will boast, saying, 'I have peace though I walk in the stubbornness of my heart to destroy the watered land with the dry.' Such a person has no boundaries for his behavior. He does what he wants and rests in a false sense of saving grace. The covenant means nothing because, in his mind, he is kept no matter what he does.

In verses twenty and twenty-one, God has something different to say about such a person's salvation. "The LORD shall never be willing to forgive him, but rather the anger of the LORD and His jealousy will burn against that man, and every curse written in this book will rest on him, and the LORD will blot out his name from under heaven. "Then the LORD will single him out for adversity from all the tribes of Israel, according to all the curses of the covenant which are written in this book of the law." This kind of God is not understood under "Easy Believism."

Moses was not teaching salvation through the works of the

law in Deuteronomy twenty-nine; he was instructing the people to be honest with God. Jesus condemned hypocrisy like no other sin. He railed on religious hypocrites in Matthew 23. I fear the Church in the West is filled with hypocrisy. Pray the prayer, walk the aisle, and be baptized; nothing further is necessary.

Under the old covenant, there was the law that, like a schoolmaster, was put in place to lead sinners to a sacrificial offering for salvation. At the sacrifice, the one offering blood would place their hand upon the thing offered, acknowledging that their sins caused its death. It is at this point that repentance becomes painfully and necessarily straightforward. Without repentance, there can be no saving faith. Repentance always precedes saving faith.

Let us consider some verses. "...solemnly testifying to both Jews and Greeks of repentance toward God and faith in our Lord Jesus Christ." (Acts 20:21). "Therefore leaving the elementary teaching about the Christ, let us press on to maturity, not laying again a foundation of repentance from dead works and of faith toward God." (Hebrews 6:1) An unrepentant heart will not believe unto salvation. "O LORD, do not Your eyes look for truth? You have smitten them, but they did not weaken; You have consumed them, but they refused to take correction. They have made their faces harder than rock; they have refused to repent." (Jeremiah 5:3)" "Therefore remember from where you have fallen, and repent and do the deeds you did at first; or else I am coming to you and will remove your lampstand out of its place— unless you repent." (Revelation 2:5) "But someone may well say, "You have faith and I have works; show me your faith without the works, and I will show you my faith by my works." (James 2:18) "Paul said, "John baptized with the baptism of repentance, telling the people to believe in Him who was coming after him, that is, in Jesus." (Acts 19:4) "but kept declaring both to those of Damascus first, and also at Jerusalem and then throughout all the region of Judea, and even to the Gentiles, that they should repent and turn to God, performing deeds appropriate to repentance." (Acts 26:20) Many more verses could be cited, but I hope my readers have gotten the scriptural mandate.

## Israel's Apostasy

Under the leadership of Joshua, there is godliness in Israel. As a result, the people and the land prospered, as seen in Judges 2:7. "The people served the LORD all the days of Joshua, and all the days of the elders who survived Joshua, who had seen all the great work of the LORD which He had done for Israel." Unfortunately, when Joshua and all his generation passed, their history and moral status also disappeared. "All that generation also were gathered to their fathers; and another generation rose up after them who did not know the LORD, nor even the work which He had done for Israel."

It is the responsibility of every generation to perpetuate

that which is godly, reasonable, and honorable so that future generations can experience the same kind of prosperity. The first generation in Israel did not successfully pass on the good news of God's salvation. "Then the sons of Israel did evil in the sight of the LORD and served the Baals, and they abandoned the LORD, the God of their fathers, who had brought them out of the land of Egypt, and they followed other gods from the gods of the peoples who were around them, and bowed down to them; so they provoked the LORD to anger. They abandoned the LORD and served Baal and the Ashtaroth. Then the anger of the LORD burned against Israel, and He handed them over to plunderers, and they plundered them; and He sold them into the hands of their enemies around them, so that they could no longer stand against their enemies." (Judges 2:11-14)

## Where were the Shepherds?

In Israel, at the time of Moses and following, the men designated to look after the religious interests of the nation were the tribe of Levi, who were the priests of the people. The priests were to intercede for the people to God and for God to the people. There is the story of Micah, who hired a Levite as his priest.

After him, there is the sorted story of a Levite who had a wife and concubine or someone he slept with but whom he did not marry. Men of a particular town rape and kill his concubine, so he cuts her into twelve pieces and sends her to the twelve tribes of Israel.

When the next generation grew up and replaced those who conquered the land, they absorbed all the ways of the surrounding people groups, became idolaters, corrupted their ways, and no longer enjoyed the blessings of God in themselves or on their land.

When Israel rebelled by sinning and desired to worship a golden calf against God under Aaron, Moses returned. The account is in Exodus 32:25-26, "Now when Moses saw that the people were out of control—for Aaron had let them get out of control to be a derision among their enemies— then Moses stood in the gate of the camp, and said, "Whoever is for the LORD, come to me!" And all the sons of Levi gathered together to him." We do not read of a subsequent account of the Levites taking a stand as they did under Moses. That generation died with those who fell in the wilderness wandering.

Israel's history is filled with compromises and eventually rejecting God in favor of an earthly king like all the other nations. God raised judges and prophets of His choosing. The kings were a lineage of primarily ungodly men who led Israel into repeated idolatry. The priesthood, as did the judges and prophets, never took a stand for God. Samuel was unlike the priesthood; we read about one such time in 1 Samuel 16:4, "So Samuel did what the LORD said, and came to Bethlehem. And the city elders came trembling to meet him and said, "Do you come in peace?"

We are taught in Proverbs 29:25, "The fear of man brings

a snare, But he who trusts in the LORD will be exalted." The Apostasy in Israel has also occurred in the Church; as Israel was warned, the Church has been warned in the book of Revelation in many other places, as in Acts 20:24-38.

## The Church has been Warned of Apostasy

In Acts chapter 20, Paul sent for the elders at Ephesus to come to him at Miletus, and when they arrived, he reviewed what kind of a shepherd he had been to them. "Therefore, I testify to you this day that I am innocent of the blood of all men. "For I did not shrink from declaring to you the whole purpose of God." On the surface, Paul may seem to say that he proclaimed all the doctrines. Still, in reality, he declared them correctly. When he says, "the whole purpose of God," he meant he did not leave anything out because it might scare some people, confuse others, or infuriate still more.

After remembering his work comes the warning for them and us today. "Be on guard for yourselves and for all the flock, among which the Holy Spirit has made you overseers, to shepherd the church of God which He purchased with His own blood." Being on your guard means being aware of the state of others and ourselves. It is all too easy to assume all is well for various reasons when, in fact, it is nothing of the sort.

Then, he makes explicit what was about to come upon the Church and continues today in a much-expanded way. "I know that after my departure savage wolves will come in among you, not sparing the flock; and from among your own selves men will arise, speaking perverse things, to draw away the disciples after them." Understand the revelatory statement Paul made to them. Some men aimed to draw people after themselves, that is, instead of following Christ.

The word for perverse in the NAS is *diastrépho* turned into a new shape that is "*distorted or twisted.*" For example, it is "opposite" from the shape or form it *should* be. It is twisted in two and corrupt." It might not sound twisted or distorted to the hearers because the devil can be a very subtle liar.

There is no doubt that many men in ministry are unaware of the corruption of the Gospel that they pass along. For men, naive but well-meaning young converts, they attend the school where they are sent, sit in awe at the very learned men who hold PhDs, and assume more often than not, even though all kinds of discussions erupt in class and out. Ultimately, the particular seminary has the key to what and how they teach. Do they include all the arguments from five hundred years of debate and confusion? Are the confessions reviewed and carefully considered in light of the scriptures, and are they given the weight they should? If all seminaries were fair the way they should be and the Holy Spirit were permitted to be the Lord of the word He authored, all regenerated and well-saved students would agree. The Holy Spirit is clear, and He would never tell one student one thing and another something different.

# Shepherds are not for Hire

When believers follow Jesus Christ, they instinctively begin to know that more is desired of them than life as it once was. All are called to invest in the lives of others and not just people who feel called to "ministry." Jesus Christ shed His precious blood for every disciple given Him by the Father. Such a sacrifice demands a deep sense of responsibility from all who call themselves His.

Having stated the responsibility of all the members of Christ's body, let us begin by being gracious to the shepherds. Every shepherd wants his flock to be well-fed, protected from harm, and prosper as Jesus Christ's disciples. Jesus did not start in such a gracious place when he said in John 10:11-13.

"I am the good shepherd; the good shepherd lays down His life for the sheep. "He who is a hired hand, and not a shepherd, who is not the sheep's owner, sees the wolf coming, leaves the sheep and flees, and the wolf snatches them and scatters them. "He flees because he is a hired hand and is not concerned about the sheep."

Jesus, Paul, and all the Apostles laid down their lives for the sheep. Many good men in history did not endure martyrdom, but undoubtedly, they were willing. False prophets are in it for the pay, according to Jesus. Again, in Matthew 7:15, Jesus said, "Beware of the false prophets, who come to you in sheep's clothing, but inwardly are ravenous wolves."

Like everyone in a particular line of work, a shepherd

partakes of the goods available to him. For this reason, Jesus said, "Who come to you in sheep's clothing." They look like shepherds; they may even think they are a shepherd, but Jesus knows they are not. While living in Michigan and an intern at a church, I visited another church and met a pastor who shared his testimony about getting saved preaching his sermon. Think of it: After thinking of himself as a Christian, he attended seminary, began pastoring a church, and yet was not even in the Kingdom of God. The good part of the story is that he recognized the most important part of his life was missing - his rebirth.

There are no doubt many reasons a person decides to go into "ministry." The pastor or shepherd is tasked with helping a flock mature. Maturing will include teaching and counseling, but all the work comes under "Go make disciples." A disciple is a follower of Jesus Christ. We only follow more mature believers as they follow Jesus Christ; anything else is idolatrous.

Upon meeting every person who has attended Church, when they begin to tell me about their Church, they always say, "Our pastor is excellent; he preaches right from the Bible." I'm going out on a limb here to say I never hear a particular doctrine taught, let alone correctly explained. The teaching I reference is the most vital in all Christian doctrines.

## Absentee Shepherds

What does a church need an elder to be? According to Acts

14:23, we read, "When they had appointed elders for them in every church, having prayed with fasting, they commended them to the Lord in whom they had believed." Sometimes, Paul stayed in one place for years, and at other times, he left the Church he planted to prosper by the grace of God without him. We know what Paul, by the inspiration, desired in an elder from his letters to Timothy and Titus.

However, what is required of men today? Much of what I have written thus far, I know, is negative, but my personal experience with the Church has been much of the same. Many friendly, well-meaning, trained, and professional men fill the pulpits in America. Preaching is the means of growing a church. Nonetheless, what makes a good preacher?

E. M. Bounds once wrote, "That it doesn't take twenty hours to make a sermon, it takes twenty years because it takes twenty years to make a man." I would expound upon that thought by saying it takes more than years to make a man of God. In the Acts passage above, we read that they fasted; to fast can take days, depending upon how many meals you miss. If the Church then did more of any one thing, it was to pray. God must bring the man to prayer to make him a man of God.

Several months ago, I was at a ministry meeting where a pastor led devotions. During the time he spoke, the pastor admitted he did not pray. He didn't say he needed to pray more; he said he didn't. The writer of Hebrews teaches us to "Remember those who led you, who spoke the word of God to you; and considering the result of their way of life, imitate their faith." (13:7)

The church leaders should have had time to mature in the faith. The faith is what the Bible teaches as a different way of life from that of the world. Hebrews tells us above that we are to consider the result of their way of life, which means consider if they are, in fact, leading a godly life. If they are, then and only then should we follow their faith or in what they are placing their trust. Godly people always pray. Pretentious people can look godly, but if they are not praying, they are not. How can I make such a statement? We are told from Romans chapter one that the just shall live by faith. No man without praying lives by faith because the most sincere form of trust in God is to pray. It is too easy to confuse morality with godliness. To live godly is to live in the presence of God.

*The man not depending upon God to build His Church is not godly. It is personal opinion, even if verses are used, that matters, but a correct and more critical Biblical view that gives Jesus Christ the final say. A godly man is first and foremost humble – a John the Baptist. A proud man is less likely to give his life away, and the shepherd gives his life to the sheep. He does not seek applause on a Sunday morning. He must say things that will upset the fleshly. He must be willing to separate the goats from the sheep so Christ's Church may be pure. These qualities are not negotiable in a shepherd, and an MDiv cannot compensate for what is lacking.*

Let me conclude this subchapter by listing the things necessary to lead a church.

Church Leaders Must:

1. Pray for a minimum of an hour a day, which does not include reading the scriptures.
2. Prayer should never be intercession only but must include Worship, Thanksgiving, Praise, Confession, and Intercession.
3. Humble themselves daily before the throne of God.
4. Acknowledge daily they cannot change anyone's heart.
5. Acknowledge daily they cannot teach anyone as if they were the source of knowledge.
6. See themselves as a channel through whom God works and nothing more.
7. An elder can disciple a group but should not only teach in a group.
8. Disciple some men one at a time with total transparency.
9. When discipling, teach the sinfulness of men, justification, identification, sanctification, Assurance, glorification, calling, and the sovereignty of God.
10. Study church history, learn the theological battles won and lost, and know the Biblical side.
11. Not be denominational with all their built-in divisions.
12. See outside the traditional boxes that enslave men in the division, justification of church compromises, worldliness, and pride.

13. Understand the difference between knowledge for knowledge's sake (pride) and knowledge that glorifies the Lord alone.
14. Understand the importance of church fellowship, sharing from the word, questioning teaching for healthy purposes, and transparency over temptations, sins, and weaknesses. (The Church must come together and walk in the (Light).
15. Understand the Assurance of salvation apart from which there cannot be a Gospel of grace.
16. Be able to fight a spiritual battleship with the enemy. (Must believe in spiritual warfare Biblically)
17. Not worship the things of the world, such as Intellectualism, spiritualism, legalism, license to evil, materialism, egotism (as a leader or any kind), or immorality.
18. Pursue a life of faith.
19. Put to death all compromise in whatever form it may appear.
20. Put to death the lust of the eyes, the lust of the flesh, and the pride of life daily.
21. Focus often upon the cross and the only means of overcoming evil.
22. Exalt the resurrection of the Lord Jesus Christ as the only head of the Church.

# Concluding Comments

This chapter is, without a doubt, the book's most negative for a reason. I am not saying there are no good churches in America, but they are hard to find. If they were so hard to find in Israel, why would it be hard to believe America might be in the same way? I will place the American Church in seven categories and decrease the number of churches closer to number seven.

1. Entertainment-driven, loud music is worship, and the pastor is everything to the Church; in the eyes of the membership, he can walk on water.
2. Emotional, doctrinally on a spectrum of fair to midland, driven by excitement and the thought that God does miracles as a regular part of life.
3. Small, friendly, entertaining, event-driven, single pastor, weak doctrinally, knowing nearly nothing of church history and the battles won
4. Ever striving for more knowledge, conceited in their understanding of the Bible and history, pastor-driven, pride in their refusal to comply with modern music, family life may be strong, but fellowship is sadly lacking.
5. Strong discipleship emphasis but short on success because of overdependence upon pastoral preaching
6. A consistent emphasis on evangelism, foreign missions, and discipleship, prayer is at a fair level at best.
7. Discipleship is at the highest level because all members

realize their responsibility before Jesus Christ. The highest motivation in all activities and fellowship is always prayer. Prayer continually drives the Church to higher levels in its love for God, His will, a love for one another, a willingness to call sin, sin in love, and a desire to restore one another.

The most profitable pastors are those who create the environment for discipleship and turn dormant pew sitters into workers sent into God's harvest field. Emotions should never lead the Church but must fill each believer's heart as the Holy Spirit moves them. Education must energize people to live in practical ways for Christ by making obedient choices in the hardest Biblical warnings, which should never be ignored.

# A. W. Tozer Quote

"For a long time, I have believed that truth, to be understood, must be believed. That doctrine of the Bible is wholly ineffective until it has been digested and assimilated by the total life. The essence of my belief is that there is a difference, a vast difference, between fact and truth. Truth in the Bible is more than a fact. A fact may be detached, cold, impersonal, and totally dissociated from life. Truth, on the other hand, is warm, living, and spiritual.

A theological fact may be held in the mind for a lifetime without its having any positive effect upon a person's moral character. The devil is a better theologian than any of us and is a devil still. Truth is creative, saving, and transforming, and it always changes the one receiving it into a holier and humbler man.

Theological facts are like the altar of Elijah on Mt. Carmel before the fire of God came - correct, properly laid out, but altogether cold. When the heart makes the ultimate surrender, the fire falls, and true facts are transmuted into spiritual truth that transforms, enlightens, and cleanses. The individual not taught the truth of God by the Spirit of God has failed to see that the truth lies deeper than the theological statement of it. At what point, then, does a theological fact become, for the one who holds it, a life-giving truth? ...at the point where faith and obedience begin."

# Chapter 6

## Sunday School or Assembly
### What is a Normal Church?

"When anyone hears the message about the kingdom and does not understand it, the evil one comes and snatches away what was sown in their heart. This is the seed sown along the path.... But the seed falling on good soil refers to someone who hears the word and understands it. This is the one who produces a crop, yielding a hundred, sixty or thirty times what was sown." Matthew 13:19, 23

## Ekklesia is More than a Preaching Ministry

Preaching is the clear teaching of the Bible, and the clear message of history, and everything that is laid out in this chapter should be understood against that backdrop. If you want to see the church spring up in a particular place, there is nothing more important or effective that you can do than to support the clear, concise preaching of the "message of the kingdom." To use a metaphor from life, the clear preaching of the Word of God is as essential and normative to the genesis of a local assembly as the act of marital intimacy is to the conception of children.

But if the Scriptures teach us that we ought to acknowledge God's control over the conception of natural children (Genesis 29:31, 30:22-23; Exodus 13:2, 34:19; 1 Samuel 1:5-6), then how much more clear is His primacy over "children born not of blood, nor of the desire or will of man, but born of God." John 1:13.

The teaching office is worthy of all due honor because the Word is worthy of the highest honor. But let us be clear: the teaching office is like a man who is given a bag of seed and commanded to sow it. His duty is not to adulterate the seed either with dust (that is, with useless additions). Neither is it his responsibility to add thorns (with counterproductive sources to the gospel) and to go out and do the hot, sweaty work of sowing out there in the heat of the day.

So, we can say that a "teaching ministry" or a structure that physically, legally, and financially facilitates the regular preaching of the Word is good and biblical? But is that structure, without more, an ekklesia? Or, if we could bring the first-century Christians forward to see our meetings, would they recognize the activity we were doing as an ekklesia or as something else?

It's important to note that Ekklesia had a clear, well-established definition in the first century. It was a legal definition as the activity of an Ekklesia was highly regulated in the first century. The right to assemble was viewed with great suspicion in Rome, as evidenced by the following quote from one of the premier Roman lawyers and statesmen of the First Century:

"If people assemble for a common purpose, whatever name we give them, and for whatever reason, they soon turn into a political club." Pliny the Younger

## Ekklesia is without a Singular Authority

Political clubs being of great concern to the Emperor, virtually all ekklesias in the Roman Empire were tightly bound to a specific purpose, either the business of a particular house or Roman noble, trade associations, worship of one of the state-approved Gods, or (for the very poor) burial associations. Burial associations served as a sort of cooperative insurance program, allowing the poor to be buried in compliance with the religious demands of their specific sect or cult.

Interestingly, many, and perhaps a majority of the early churches, were legally organized as burial assemblies, giving some more context to the Catholic and Orthodox focus on death and burial rituals. In many cases, every time the church met, they would need at least ostensibly to practice burial rituals as a cover for their actual meeting. Otherwise, they would be an illegal assembly.

The key distinction of an Ekklesia was that it was a place

for dealing with problems without an established hierarchy or authority. That means it would make no sense for someone to say that a particular person was the "head" of an ekklesia. If there was a head, an authority, someone whose word could be obeyed, then that was not an Ekklesia. See, Rome was very familiar and very comfortable with hierarchies. If there was a single dominant head, Rome was confident in its ability to bribe, threaten or otherwise control that head. But an Ekklesia, which by definition lacked a singular authority, was much more troublesome for Rome to control.

Turning to the Bible, the most obvious text for this is Acts 19, which discusses the teaching ministry of Paul in two different venues: the Synagogue of Ephesus and the School of Tyrannus. The Synagogue is derived from two words, syn or sun, which means "with," and ago, which means to bring, so the literal meaning is to "bring with." The root word synago is used for livestock or grains brought into the barn. The word translated school, or lecture hall, is schole in Greek, from which we derive the modern term for school. Schole means "leisure" or "to sit," and it implies a group of people sitting and listening.

Both of these word structures create an expectation of a passive audience. In theory, the Synagogue had a mechanism allowing new teachers from outside the city to present their views and teachings. But when Paul took advantage of this to preach the gospel, he would sooner or later be ejected from the Synagogue. In Ephesus, it appears that it was sooner rather than later and to the point where he needed to recruit more qualified men trained in the law to start an ekklesia immediately. Such ignorance left him with the task of training the existing converts he had from the ground up. In other cities, it appears that the men and women who joined Paul from the Synagogue or local Jewish community were able to begin discipling others within weeks or months.

But in Ephesus, the people who converted could NOT simply form into an Ekklesia within a short period. From the content of the Epistle of Ephesians, it would appear that the problem had something to do with a lack of physical heritage or status. Ephesians is a church of orphans, of unfathered men, which is why Paul has to spend so much time with them and why Ephesians gives so much more detail on the foundations of the church than other epistles.

So Paul had a challenge: to 1. develop mature believers who could serve as Elders and 2. spiritually feed and disciple the flock of converts gathered while those leaders were becoming qualified. Paul's method to solve this problem was to start a school.

There are two things that we can infer from this. 1. There is nothing inherently wrong with pursuing starting a school. 2. A school (or teaching ministry) is a means to correct a specific failure in the existing religious community. Once that specific failure is corrected, the formal school is replaced by an ekklesia.

So if we brought someone from the first century forward,

they would look at our services and be very encouraged by the strength of our schools. A single pastor teaching a group seated at leisure is a school. As we JUST SAW in the passage, Paul taught at a school for two years. What's so interesting is that nowhere in Acts 19 are the Christians in Ephesians called the church.

They ARE believers, they ARE disciples, they ARE coming and listening to Paul teach, but they are NOT an assembly or ekklesia. They are NOT A CHURCH. Not yet.

Now, there is an ekklesia mentioned in Acts 19. Its members are the worshippers of Artemis, who, in some vague sense, realize that Paul's teaching is undermining their cultural hegemony in the city. So they do what ekklesias do; they assemble and march to the center of town to demand action. The ekklesia is quite a flagrant violation of standing Roman law regarding assemblies. Still, the city clerk, who likely is politically connected with the Artemis cult, notes that it will violate the law if they don't disperse. But make no mistake, the Church of Artemis was a powerful functioning ekklesia with tremendous political clout.

An Ekklesia was not a place without rank, particularly in the Roman Empire. Indeed, it was strongly discouraged, among other things, for barbarians and Scythians to be treated the same as Greeks and Romans. Distinctions between males and females were ignored, and it was illegal for slaves and freemen to eat from the same table and drink from the same cup. Against this backdrop of unequal treatment enshrined in custom and law,

Paul's dramatic statements in Galatians 3:28 and Colossians 3:11 made the Christian Ekklesia the most egalitarian organization in the empire. Essentially, no distinctions of rank are left.

There are still leadership structures, Elders, Deacons, etc., but the emphasis to the First Century audience would have been on the radical equality of the Christian Ekklesia. Greco-Roman culture had not seen anything like this outside the most ancient myths. It is critical to note that this equality in one space (the ekklesia) DID NOT eliminate or downplay the roles and distinctions in marriage or household/business. There is no conflict between Paul's declaration of near-absolute equality in the church and his commands that wives submit to their husbands and children to obey their parents.

In Acts 19, there was leadership in the Ekklesia of Artemis, a key agitator, Demetrius, the silversmith, whose business was intimately involved in worshiping Artemis. After his initial speech, Demetrius fades into the background and does not appear involved in the chanting mob. His absence from criminal prosecution, after all, he didn't say anything that would dishonor Rome in his speech. Again, the town clerk is probably also a devotee of Artemis, but he can 'dismiss' the crowd without holding anyone responsible. This "soft power" is how Assemblies used to skirt the laws of the Roman Empire and why the ranking elite was suspicious of them.

So we have contrasted two types of organizations, hierarchical and non-hierarchical, and Ephesus demonstrates both righteous and unrighteous examples of both. So first, we have the unrighteous hierarchy of the Synagogue, which throws Paul out and tries to stop him from teaching. There is a clear hierarchy here, with the power to allow Paul to teach and the power to throw him out on the street.

Paul immediately forms his hierarchy, the righteous hierarchy. He goes to the lecture hall of Tyrannus and teaches for two years, raising the men who would later become elders. However, the text of Acts always refers to the "believers" or the "disciples" but NEVER to the "church" (ekklesia). Throughout this period, extreme spiritual warfare culminated in the Sons of Sceva incident and the burning of 50,000 drachmae (the modern equivalent would be about $10,000,000.00) worth of sorcerous scrolls. (Acts 19:11-20)

Finally, we see the unrighteous, non-hierarchical organization, the Ekklesia of Artemis, who rises and is dismissed by the city clerk. After this defeat, the text STILL refers to the "disciples," and then Paul departs. (Acts 20:1) Only after Paul leaves does the text start referring to the Ephesian believers as a church with Elders. (Acts 20:17)

Men eligible to be elders are always necessary. So again, preaching ministries or giving them their biblical name, Schools, are good and valuable institutions. They are essential when there is a lack of qualified upright men who can serve as elders, and their primary purpose is to raise such honorable men. So, there is nothing inherently wrong or improper with the hierarchical, scholastic form of the church.

But also, based on this passage, we must insist on the distinctions made by the text being given their full force. Namely, a school is not a church. An institution may have believers in it, and it may accurately preach the message, but this, without more, is NOT a church.

So, what is an ekklesia? An ekklesia is a group of equals meeting to decide to carry out a specific agenda. It is a group of people with resources who are gathered to tackle problems beyond their individual capacities. So, an Ekklesia does not produce resources; they require them.

Now, we must insist that an Assembly is the natural and logical outcome of a teaching ministry, in the same way that a child is the natural and logical outcome of marital intimacy. Therefore, Paul referred to himself as a father to these churches. But Paul's relationship with these churches was seen as part of the generative miracle; it was not the normative life of the church. Indeed, the command of Christ himself was that his disciples were NOT to call one another teacher or father.

So, what is the distinction between a hierarchical school and a non-hierarchical church? Well, we go back to the text of Acts 19. The progression goes something like this: Paul, the unambiguous father/teacher of the school, teaches his people. Paul does miracles, and others start doing miracles "in the name of Paul." The common thread throughout this period is that everything is done in Paul's name.

Again, it's essential to realize that this is not bad; miracles are happening, and God's spirit is being poured out. This ministry is incredibly positive and beneficial.

But God has more for these people. So, in his providence, he allows one of the demons to make clear that Jesus is primary and Paul only secondary. Therefore, the first step toward a genuine assembly is the fear of God.

Successful preachers have long known that the initial goal or the initial mark of success in preaching is the spread among people of widespread reverence, awe, and fear of God. What is fascinating to me in this passage is that this fear results from God's miraculous intervention and NOT from the teaching ministry that Paul presumably did. But in BOTH cases, God controls the genesis of new life. A church forms when empowered children of God associate in supernatural ways. The most essential of these ways is **regular, fervent, corporate prayer**.

# Chapter 7

## A HOUSE OF PRAYER
### Building through Prayer

### The Divine Declaration of Prayer

On a day ordained by the divine trinity, Christ walked into the temple. We are given the details in Mark 11:15, 16. "Then they came to Jerusalem. And He entered the temple and began to drive out those who were buying and selling in the temple, and overturned the tables of the money-changers and the seats of those who were selling doves, and He would not permit anyone to carry merchandise through the temple."

Experts tell us that a crowd of 400,000 could occupy the temple on Jesus' day. Think about how you would go about emptying a football stadium with 400,00 people in it. Roman guards would have been present to prevent revolt. Jesus could only have halted the temple activity by a miracle. It was essential to know who was doing the speaking. Jesus was no mere man.

Jesus cleansing the temple is in all four Gospel accounts.

Matthew, Mark, and Luke describe the cleansing during the Passion week at the end of Jesus' earthly ministry. In chapter two, John records the first cleansing directly after His first miracle when He turned water into wine. John begins verse twelve by using the word "with," which in Greek as an active word (metá) looks towards the after-effect (change, result), which is only defined by the context. The immediate context we are told in verse eleven is, "This beginning of [His] signs Jesus did in Cana of Galilee, and manifested His glory, and His disciples believed in Him."

Jesus left Cana, and we see Him in the temple a few days following. "And He began to teach and say to them, "Is it not written, 'MY HOUSE SHALL BE CALLED A HOUSE OF PRAYER FOR ALL THE NATIONS?' But you have made it a DEN OF THIEVES" (Mark 11:17). According to Jesus, His Father's house was to be known for prayer. Are our worship buildings today known for prayer or primarily for preaching, singing, or entertainment? Preaching is a primary way to build the body; singing is terrific for raising our voices together in a unified way to glorify God. However, what God wants to hear, first of all, is prayer.

**God is never more present than when we pray. By present, I mean never more pleased to be there.**

# The Divine Mandate to Pray

As the nineteenth century drew close, Edward McKendree Bounds reminded the Church of his day to pray. In his book Power Through Prayer, he remembered the great preachers of bygone years who became known as much for their praying as their preaching. Eight volumes in all, he called the Church to pray as its primary responsibility. Consider this blurb from The Necessity of Prayer.

"…With prayer, though the house of God might be supposed to lack everything else, it becomes a Divine sanctuary. So the Tabernacle, moving about from place to place, became the holy of holies because prayer was there. Without prayer, the building may be costly, perfect in all its appointments, beautiful for the situation, and attractive to the eye. Still, it comes down to the human, with nothing Divine in it, and is on a level with all other buildings.

Without prayer, a church is like a body without Spirit; it is a dead, inanimate thing. A church with prayer in it has God in it. When prayer is set aside, God is outlawed. When prayer becomes an unfamiliar exercise, then God Himself is a stranger there.

…While it is conceded that preaching of the Word has an important place in the house of God. Yet, prayer is its predominant distinguishing feature.

…The work belonging to other places is done without

special reference to God. He is not specifically recognized nor called upon. In the Church, however, God is acknowledged, and nothing is done without Him. Prayer is the distinguishing mark of the house of God. As prayer distinguishes Christians from unchristian people, so prayer distinguishes God's house from all other houses. It is a place where faithful believers meet with their Lord.

...As God's house is a house where the business of praying is carried on, so is it a place where the business of making praying people out of prayerless people is done. The house of God is a Divine workshop, and there, the work of prayer goes on. Or the house of God is a divine schoolhouse, in which the lesson of prayer is taught, where men and women learn to pray, and where they graduate in the school of prayer.

Any church calling itself the house of God and failing to magnify prayer, which does not put prayer in the forefront of its activities, which does not teach the great lesson of prayer, should change its teaching to conform to the Divine pattern or change the name of its building to something other than a house of prayer." E. M. Bounds

## The Divine Example of Praying

My dear readers, all of us who have received Jesus Christ as Lord have entered a battlefield of the soul. We are born again into this war with the world, the flesh, and the devil. All we have for our protection is the armor of God. It is vital protection against a heartless, savage, and ruthless enemy. When armed with God's promises, we are protected. "Greater is He that is in you, then he that is in the world."

When we find our identity in Christ, we put on our armor. We put on our armor when we relinquish control, pray, and trust in Him. When we pray, we put on our armor and become God's house instead of thinking it's His while usurping His power and authority.

Prayer is practicing the presence of God. Those who do not pray do not experience the presence of God. Jesus was constantly aware of God's presence as a human being. Nonetheless, Jesus made it a practice to pray. Why? Through prayer, Jesus identified with the human race's need to pray so that members of the human race could identify with Him.

The book of Hebrews best explains the highly priestly ministry of Jesus. The Christian who rightly understands the ministry of prayer sees Jesus on His knees there as our Great High Priest. "For we do not have a high priest who cannot sympathize with our weaknesses, but One who has been tempted in all things as we are, yet without sin." (Hebrews 4:15)

Jesus humbled himself in the days of His weakness. "Who, in the days of His flesh, when He had offered up prayers and supplications, with vehement cries and tears to Him who was able to save Him from death, and was heard because of His godly fear." (Hebrews 5:7) Let us then go to Him in prayer, for we will find Him there as one who understands our condition. "Therefore let us draw near with confidence to the throne of grace, so that we may receive mercy and find grace to help in time of need" (Hebrews 4:16).

Over the years, I have brought men together to pray during the early morning watch from 3 A.M. to 8:30. On at least five occasions, we had as many as sixteen men. There were numerous reasons for these prayer sessions, which we will look into shortly. People clamored to attend, but that would not be true. On one occasion, when inviting a pastor of a sister church, he told me. "You want to pray at 3 A.M.? If I do, I'll fall asleep."

When asking an old friend and retired pastor, "How would you have responded, as a pastor, if a brother asked you to come out in the early morning to pray?" He responded, "I would have climbed up on my desk and started to dance." Dear pastors, if you are not taking your calling seriously to pray, please consider the following verses as a mandate to your ministry.

1. "It was at this time that He went off to the mountain to pray, and He spent the whole night in prayer to God" (Luke 6:12).
2. "In the early morning, while it was still dark, Jesus got up, left the house, and went away to a secluded place, and was praying there" (Mark 1:35).
3. "These all with one mind were continually devoting themselves to prayer, along with the women, and Mary, the mother of Jesus, and with His brothers." (Acts 1:14).

4. "They were continually devoting themselves to the apostles' teaching and to fellowship, to the breaking of bread and to prayer. Everyone kept feeling a sense of awe..." (Acts 2:42, 43).

5. "And when they had prayed, the place where they had gathered together was shaken, and they were all filled with the Holy Spirit and began to speak the word of God with boldness" (Acts 4:31).

6. "Now there was a man at Caesarea named Cornelius, a centurion of what was called the Italian cohort, a devout man and one who feared God with all his household, and gave many alms to the Jewish people and prayed to God continually." (Acts 10:1, 2)

7. "When they had appointed elders for them in every church, having prayed with fasting, they commended them to the Lord in whom they had believed" (Acts 14:23).

8. "With all prayer and petition pray at all times in the Spirit, and with this in view, be on the alert with all perseverance and petition for all the saints." (Ephesians 6:18)

9. "Pray without ceasing." (1 Thessalonians 5:17)

10. "Therefore I want the men in every place to pray, lifting up holy hands, without wrath and dissension." (1 Timothy 2:8)

There is a devotion in the previous verses, a resolution to

pray that far exceeds duty and obligation. So much has been said and written about loving God, but what person loves God and does not take time, real-time, to pray?

Jesus was Almighty God in the flesh, and He rose from His comfortable bed a great while before morning light and prayed. Jesus even prayed throughout the entire night. Have you ever done that? I tell you, there is nothing like it.

In Acts 1:14, the writer uses a serious term to describe how the people prayed, "...continually devoting themselves...", which correctly interpreted means to consistently show strength which prevails, despite difficulties." When you rise at 3 A.M. to pray, you'd better be able to prevail. You will need to know what it takes to pray in the Spirit, and I do not mean only emotionally.

## The Divine Fruit of Prayer

In the first three Gospels, before entering Jerusalem and reproaching the people for turning His Father's house into a den of thieves, there is the incident with the fig tree that Jesus cursed because it had no fruit. It is true it was not the season for figs, and the point is that God has the right and the authority to do what He will with His creation.

The following day, they all recognized the tree being rotten from the roots up. It was wholly withered like it had become that way over a more extended time. Jesus had in mind to teach His followers an essential lesson on prayer. He said to them,

"Have faith in God. "Truly I say to you; whoever says to this mountain, 'Be taken up and cast into the sea,' and does not doubt in his heart, but believes that what he says is going to happen, it will be granted him. "Therefore, I say to you, all things for which you pray and ask, believe that you have received them, and they will be granted you" (Mark 11:22-24).

There is praying in the Spirit, which means it is first in tune with God. God's will becomes preeminent. Second, it goes beyond the limits of just saying words; it reaches heaven, and God reaches back. We are now in the realm of faith. "For whatever is born of God overcomes the world; and this is the victory that has overcome the world—our faith" (1 John 5:4). What overcomes the world? God! God overcomes the world; the means He uses within us is our trust in Him, thus faith.

We must overcome an obstacle to exercise the kind of faith we receive from God; it is the obstacle to God's will. "This is the confidence which we have before Him, that, if we ask anything according to His will, He hears us" (1 John 5:14). This place is the devil's playground, nothing other than the elusive will of God. All we need to do is question if our request is God's will, and all faith is gone. Nonetheless, we must pray in the will of God. The will of God and faith come together when we walk in the Spirit, and God's will becomes our conviction.

When these two elements come together, we can know God hears us. To be heard by God is no small matter. God knows everything and is everywhere, so He hears everything. However, that is different from what John is referring to here. In verse fourteen, there is a confidence that a person has who knows they possess eternal life. Referring back to verse thirteen, John wrote the letter so that the person who believed in Jesus unto salvation might know they had eternal life. The confidence with which believers speak proceeds from God-given discernment. "My sheep hear my voice, I know them, and they follow me" (John 10:27). The relationship is reciprocal.

In other words, God recognizes those who belong to Him. God knows intimately and loves those who follow Him. They follow Him because He loves them. When His people walk in His ways, He reveals His desires to them, and they ask accordingly. "And if we know that He hears us in whatever we ask, we know that we have the requests which we have asked from Him" (1 John 5:15).

Therefore, "...whoever says to this mountain, 'Be taken up and cast into the sea,' and does not doubt in his heart, but believes that what he says is going to happen, it will be granted him...". The child of God is to live with the kind of confidence that can ask great things and, knowing it is God's will, receives them. Therefore, our Lord concludes by saying, "Therefore, I say to you, all things for which you pray and ask, believe that you have received them." Where there is no doubt, there is the fulfillment of the request.

If you are not familiar with the story of George Mueller, you should be because his experience was one of the God-fulfilling answers to prayer his whole love through. His prayers were not without the constant experience of dying to self, but his reward was a great harvest of answered prayers.

I am not teaching a health and wealth Gospel - just the Gospel. I did not say, 'Have faith in God; Jesus did! I did not say, "Whoever says to this mountain, 'Be taken up and cast into the sea,' and does not doubt in his heart, but believes that what he says is going to happen; it will be granted him" Jesus did! If you are prone to contest these things, your problem is not with me but with Jesus. However, the twisting of what Jesus said is probably not coming from you but from the devil.

## How to Pray for Hours

Ordered flexibility is the best way for people to pray together.

1. The leader casts the vision.
   a. He teaches about prayer. Never speak for more than fifteen minutes. This time is for praying, not teaching.
   b. Place the people in the position to receive God's power.
   c. Example: "How could one chase a thousand, and two put ten thousand to flight?" (Deuteronomy 32:30) In the economy of God, one chases 1,000, but two chases 10,000. God's math is not ours, so

numbers add by ten, which is why praying together is so important.

2. The leader sets the stage and then lets the Lord lead the people.
   a. If you want to pray for five hours, you will need something about which to pray.
   b. Set the parameters: (These are guidelines and not rules)
   c. An hour of praise is good. Praise is not thanksgiving because its only focus is the character of God. Thankfulness is good, but not when it detracts from praising God for what He is by making His character for our benefit.
   d. An hour of Thanksgiving is fitting. If done in humility, it will lead to the next hour.
   e. An hour of confessing sins is humbling. The Holy Spirit always leads our repentance to the cross for forgiveness and cleansing.
   f. The fourth and possibly fifth hours are for intercession for the world.
3. Pray the Scriptures.
   a. Healthy praying is praying where we leave ourselves behind.
   b. God's will is found in His Word; it does not originate from us but from Him.
   When reading God's Word during prayer, He stirs

the hearts of the one praying with a deeper and richer awareness of His presence. Allowing scripture to guide our thinking during prayer is vital to our thought life. Even in prayer, it is all too easy to swerve from God's will and get off the path of the straight and narrow. During prayer, always fill your mind with the words and will of God.

4. Conversational Praying is Relational.

   a. Set the time limits: Divide the entire time by the number of people—five times sixty equals 300 minutes. If there are twenty people, each person gets 15 minutes total, divided by four sections, which is 3.75 minutes each. One who likes to talk a lot can bring down the Spirit of the meeting. There needs to be freedom for the Spirit to lead. However, where there is the Spirit of the Lord, there is a consideration for others.

5. Pray in a Manner Pleasing to the Lord

   a. All prayer warriors need to be Spirit-Filled

   b. There is no room for show-boating

   c. The Spirit-filled believer comes to the meeting in a broken state. When we bring sin to the meeting, we ask God to leave.

   d. Sin keeps believers from spirit-filled praying like nothing else.

6. Pray for Revival
   a. Revival is something that only God can do, and He brings it to pass in His time.
   b. Revival is an outpouring of the Spirit.
   c. Where there is a revival, there is an uncommon awareness of sin.
   d. Pentecost was revival. Revival is not for self-gratification or pride; it can only happen in God's time and power. Therefore, pray for it to come.
   e. Revival brings the Church to behavior like the opening chapter of Acts.
   f. In Acts, the people shared all things in common, and no person regarded their property as their own.
   g. The outpouring of the Spirit always brings boldness to proclaim the Gospel, even to death.

When God made man in His image, He made him intellectual, emotional, willful, and able to make moral choices. During spirit-filled prayer, sanctified, saved sinners' minds, emotions, and will are governed by God. All it takes is one person to bring down the entire presence of a prayer meeting of this type. People need to be prepared for this type of prayer meeting; if you understand my meaning, the people attending need to be all in for prayer. In John eleven, we see Jesus waiting to return home for the prearranged events to occur. He was God, always submitting to the Holy Spirit's will, as they were one. He was mindful in all He chose to do. Secondly, He was always in control of His emotions. Nonetheless, He was never without emotions. "Jesus wept" (John 11:35). "So Jesus, again being deeply moved within, came to the tomb" (John 11:38). We should be so moved when we come to pray. A spirit-filled prayer meeting will always accomplish Jesus' words, will, and much more. "Jesus said to her, "Did I not say to you that if you believe, you will see the glory of God?" (John 11:40). God's glory was seen by a man's body raised from the dead, so today it can be seen as men being raised from a soulish death when God's people pray.

# Chapter 8

## THE HOUSEHOLD OF GOD
### How Brotherhood is the Essence of Piety

Then the righteous will answer Him, 'Lord, when did we see You hungry and feed You, or thirsty and give You something to drink? When did we see You a stranger and take You in, or naked and clothe You? When did we see You sick or in prison and visit You?' And the King will reply, 'Truly I tell you, whatever you did for one of the least of these brothers of Mine, you did for Me.' Mathew 24:38-40, BSB (Emphasis Added)

## Household as a Foreign Concept

*"By doing good, especially to those of the Household of faith or groaning so to be; employing them preferably to others; buying one another, helping each other in business, and so much more because the world will love its own and them only."*
– The nature, design, and general rules of the
United Societies, John Wesley, 1743

When you study the biblical words collectively translated, House, Household, dynasty, generation, lineage, tribe, clan, people, and race, you find that there is NO equivalent word in modern English that you can use to translate this concept adequately. Even by the low standards of modern Bible translators, race is a spectacularly bad judgment. No equivalent word in modern English is partly why we have difficulty understanding the biblical meaning of other words, like upright man, righteous man, honorable man, a man of valor, and head of Household. Particularly significant in the New Testament context is the Elder and Brother. These words are ranks or positions within a household in the original languages.

The Biblical household concept implies a whole network of economic, relational, and spiritual concepts foreign to the modern mind. That means, as a culture, we don't have any way to evaluate whether we are following the biblical injunctions directed towards the level of relationship that I am referring to as "Household." We need to gain the conceptual vocabulary to ask the question.

Suppose the authority of Christ extends to all degrees of human activity, as discussed in Chapter 2. In that case, these ancient words, these covenants, these conceptual relational frameworks are vectors of God's blessing and grace, specifically his common grace. When a society discards one of these vectors, by definition, they lose access, at least to some degree, to that blessing. I believe American society is starting to be seriously impacted by the lack of effective households following God's covenant principles.

Effective households are particularly true when we remember that the physical command of the 10 Commandments that corresponds to the family is Do Not Steal. Modern economic science has now proven (finally catching up to the Bible) that an economy's most fundamental building block is trust, specifically trust that people will honor their deals. Who can deny that white-collar crime, theft from WITHIN an organization or structure, is a major issue in our society, from the petty theft of office supplies to massive stock-market-crashing fraud?

So that's the diagnostic part, and I hope you see what we have done here; we have connected a real current problem, theft, with an institution, a relational structure, the Household, which the Bible gives us an ENORMOUS wealth of information. It is no exaggeration to say that of our understanding of how households worked and governed themselves in the Ancient world, the Biblical texts and commentaries are likely more detailed than the rest of the preserved antiquity combined.

## Household as a Biblical Concept

So, by this point, many of you are tired of hearing what a household is NOT and would like to know what a household IS. For our purposes, here, a household performs two functions. The first function is that the Household is where the children are raised to be Yashar and Chayil, upright and virtuous. Therefore, at a physical level, the "household" is that economic entity that allows access to the things a family needs to raise children regarding food, shelter, clothing, medical care, skills training, intellectual instruction, and spiritual formation. Some cultures provide easy access to some of these things, at the BIBLICAL QUALITY STANDARD, in their open markets, at a price point within the means of one married couple. No culture I am aware of provides access to all of them in the quality the Bible would accept.

Suppose we are fantasizing about some Libertarian Utopia. In that case, I will freely grant that if we had a just and fair legal system, honest weights and measures, etc., one married couple likely WOULD have sufficient economic purchasing power to access these things and provide them to their children. But in the world in which we live, people must come together and gather enough people to allow them to act as a Company or a Firm, engaging in collective bargaining with the market to get these goods or services at a quality that meets the Biblical standard.

To successfully continue to accomplish this collective bargaining over extended periods, that is, generations, households are going to come together around upright men who are succeeding in business. But the focus is not any specific going concern; it is on the relationships between the family members that make the company go. The Old Testament language is framed in terms of Fathers, Sons, and Brothers. The idea is that if you can have Biblically healthy Father-Son relationships and Brother-Brother relationships, you will be able to solve any particular economic challenge and keep the family name and business going.

Business relationships are all physical, of course. The spiritual household steps into the gap where the physical households fail: "Though my father and mother forsake me, the LORD will receive me." [Psalm 27:10](https://biblehub.com/psalms/27-10. htm). Whatever the physical Household was unable to do, whatever mishap it allowed in that prevented them from standing up straight as Upright Sons and Daughters, the spiritual Household, the spiritual Father is supernaturally empowered to remove.

But the second function is that households are also places for more extensive covenant responsibilities. The idea is that resources follow obligations, and responsibilities are placed on Covenants. Right now, in America, we only think covenantally about marriage. And that means we are limited to duties and visions, which are small enough to be held by a single covenant of two people in marriage during their lifetime.

The solution is to start painting a broad picture of how deep and rich the covenant relationships between people can be. The Household is the primary place where the Bible explores multi-generational covenants. So if God wants something done that will take ten couples to be in covenant with each other for four generations of their descendants, that's still in the biblical "household" space. And that means we can dream big dreams that will take longer than our own lives to fulfill.

The Household is critical to both key solutions, and we must see this movement become genuinely transformative. 1. The ability to raise up, Upright[1] Sons and Daughters (either because the physical Household did its job correctly or by applying the purifying ministry of spiritual fathers). 2. The ability to "stand up"[2] and accept BIG covenant responsibilities, city-taking, involving multiple marriages and individuals coming together with a vision that will take generations to complete.

## Household Membership as Something Distinct

Household membership is something distinct. That doesn't nec-essarily mean moving into the same physical house or working for the same company. But it means a covenant right and duty to this PARTICULAR Purpose and these PARTICULAR People. It means that these people are your family and that, long-term, your normative expectation is that you are going to work for one of the family businesses and that you are going to do business FIRST with family. You will laugh with them, cry with them, and show up when they have weddings, births,

---

1 [Chayil](https://biblehub.com/hebrew/2428.htm)

2 [Amad](https://biblehub.com/hebrew/5975.htm), [2 Kings 23:3](https://biblehub.com/2_kings/23-3.htm) "and all the people [STOOD] to the covenant"

and funerals. Everyone must consider that their well-being also involves their name and house honor.

**And that hope with skin on in a broken world.** You set a table before me in the presence of my enemies.

As we seek to correct our biblical illiteracy about the house or Household, it is vitally important to examine what the ancient cultures saw as the foundational relationships that made up the Household. These were explicitly Fathers, Sons, and Brothers. Much could be said about what a Father is spiritually, biblically, and in many other ways. The subject of fatherhood and its importance to every area of life was a favorite topic of ancient writers. Duty to one's parents or filial piety was seen as the most basic, essential duties, without which any other appeals to conscience or morality would be meaningless. That is why they would have seen nothing odd in the ancient world, including "disobedient to parents" in a list of CAPITAL crimes (crimes for which the penalty was death).

But what IS a father? Well, fundamentally, a father is the one who FEEDS. That is why the central request in the Lord's prayer (literally the central, 4th out of 7) is for our daily bread. That is why when Christ wants to illustrate that God is a good father, he references giving bread instead of stone and fish instead of snakes. Feeding your children is the core definitional requirement in the ancient world for what a father was. A Father is MORE than just that; someone who does not feed his children has, in a significant way, ceased to be a father.

By implication, a Son has the right to sit and eat at his Father's table. Being a son is much more than that; it is the bare minimum, or perhaps the fundamental metaphor, of the Father and Son. A Son does not have to worry about from where his next meal comes.

In our modern food-rich society, realizing what that means may take time. But if you have ever dealt with people, say orphans from Africa or South Asia in particular, where orphan children regularly starve to death on the streets, you quickly learn that food is life, everything, and the ONLY thing.

A street kid who steals to eat cares about NOTHING else but how to get his next meal. He does not have plans; he does not have ambitions. He lives in the now, and the only thing that matters is preserving his ability to get the next meal. He is caught in the trap of hunger. That is why he will refuse baths, clean clothes, books, and anything that would impede him the next time he has to go out and steal. His familiar patterns are his lifeline; you might even say they are sacred.

Food-hoarding habits continue even once a child has been adopted, rescued, and removed from extreme deprivation. Food-hoarding habits are a sign of a fatherless child, and there is only one way to cure it. Someone must step up to the plate of fatherhood and say to that boy, "You can eat here. There is a place for you at my table, I promise."

And then, having made that promise, you must keep it, and keep it, and keep it again until the child has become so accustomed to the commitment that they never question it. The principle that there WILL BE FOOD must penetrate their souls at these times, every single day. Indeed, in a manner, the Father keeps the promise until the Son does not even think of it. And the Son does not think of the promise because they are thinking, planning, and looking long-term for the first time. They can strategize, gather resources, save, and defer gratification because their basic needs are met. What are they thinking? What are they planning? Why are they planning to accomplish the dreams and visions they receive from their Father while they sit at his table?

And THAT is what a Son is; it is someone who has a relationship with his Father, who feeds him, and therefore, he does not worry about "what he will eat or drink," but he seeks first the glory, the honor, of the Kingdom of his Father.

## Where are Our Brothers?

Our imminent collapse has been one of the perennial topics of discussion in the modern West for at least the last 40 years. While you can debate the likelihood of total economic failure or totalitarian takeover, our vulnerability is the chief reason we keep discussing these topics. As has been remarked several times, 2008 wasn't the end of THE world, but for many people, it was the end of THEIR world. And that is what we fear: the end of OUR world.

The Bible refers to this state of having lost everything as being rejected by your brothers, "by your own mother's sons." Psalm 69:8. Similarly, the Greek word for brother adelphos means 'from the womb' or the same womb. The Household, the natural and covenantal extended family, was a critically important relationship for people in the ancient world. Upon reaching middle age, while your Father would retain primacy in terms of your duty to obey when you were asking for help, you were appealing to the network of brothers and uncles who collectively composed the military might of the family. The Old Testament calls these the yashar, the "upright men." The personal cash, connections, and property of those upright men, those pillars, provided support in core areas like housing, job security, creditworthiness, and a social safety net.

To be rejected by your brothers, like the writer in Psalm 69, means that you have lost not only the immediate ability to provide for your family BUT ALSO the ability to survive until you can rebuild. In short, if your brothers have rejected you, then in human terms, that is it for you; you are done. Brothers are the ones you expect to help from until you get back on your feet again. Brothers have a duty to make you whole when they haven't done anything wrong to you, or even when you did something wrong to a third party or even to them. The Bible has a word for this, too, *chesed*, which means sacrificial love, covenant faithfulness, or loving-kindness.

Now, that sounds like a fairly scary thing, loving sacrificially.

But another way to think of it might be that brothers function as a team, and teams win or lose together. No matter how brilliant, an individual member of a basketball team or a football team cannot win while his teammates lose. They rise or fall together.

Now, that sounds like a fairly scary thing, loving sacrificially. But another way to think of it might be that brothers function as a team, and teams win or lose together. No matter how brilliant, an individual member of a basketball team or a football team cannot win while his teammates lose. They rise or fall together.

When brothers are unified and share sacrificially and lovingly, the Bible presents the natural and logical outcome of such unity as wealth and abundance. Sacrificial love is not some magical guarantee; it's how God made the world. And this is the underlying meaning of the conclusion of Psalm 133.

Again, the imagery that the first readers of this psalm would probably think of is the family farm. Subsistence farming, particularly in the ancient world, was an enterprise that required teams of men to work together. Whether lifting large beams, coordinating teams of animals, or balancing loads on a wagon, the critical take on a farm requires more than one person. "Many hands make light work" when carrying a forty-foot log was not a statement about how fast you could accomplish the task; it was about whether the job could be done.

When you have to defend your home from bandits, no matter how fierce, one man alone cannot protect the walls of even a moderately sized compound, much less the fields of a farm.

Only with 10-12 men could you begin to provide basic security in the lawless environments of the ancient world.

Further, aside from the daily tasks or dangers, brothers, in particular, are capable of long-term planning and cooperation because they don't have to worry about where their next meal is coming from and know that the rest of their brothers are similarly reliable.

Now, this is not to say that you cannot create or be a part of other teams or that you cannot love other people in a sacrificial covenantal manner. But building other groups is an extra, an added burden, and of course, when you need a team the most, it is precisely then you cannot spare any other resources.

On that day of trouble, you need people who love you not primarily for what you have done but for who you are and the name your Father gave you. In our modern-day, where family is seen as a burden, and an afterthought, the biblical language of brotherhood has little emotional force. But perhaps it is because we have forgotten our physical and spiritual brothers that we are all terrified of an impending collapse. Maybe we would do well to rediscover and honor the notion that God gave us brothers, physical and spiritual, and we rise or fall together. We may discover how good and pleasant it is when brothers dwell in unity. Because we have no sense of unity or team based on an unchanging lineage, we feel ourselves on the brink, one step from impending doom.

Some will respond, well, it is great to know that brothers

are beneficial when you have unity. But for most families, unity is precisely the problem. If fathers are supposed to be the solution, how do we overcome generations of absent, indifferent, or abusive fathering?

It is this, which is the earth-shattering good news that underlies Ephesians.

"In love, He predestined us to adoption as sons and daughters through Jesus Christ to Himself...In Him, we also have obtained an inheritance... In Him, you also, after listening to the message of truth, the gospel of your salvation—having also believed, you were sealed in Him with the Holy Spirit of the promise, who is a first installment of our inheritance, regarding the redemption of God's possession, to the praise of His glory. Ephesians 1:4b-5a, 11a, 13-14

...when you read, you can understand my insight into the mystery of Christ.... specifically, that the Gentiles are fellow heirs and fellow members of the body. Fellow partakers of the promise in Christ Jesus through the gospel ...For this reason, I bend my knees before the Father, from whom every family in heaven and on earth derives its name. Ephesians 3:4,6,14-15

It should be noted that the predestination of Ephesians 1, or more specifically, the determinism of Ephesians 1, is not being defended. No educated man in the First Century believed in free will as that term is understood in the modern era, and there is no evidence that Paul disagreed with that general sentiment. Instead, the glaring self-evident reality of Rome (where perhaps

90% of the population were outright slaves) was that people were NOT free in any meaningful sense.

Because the Roman world agreed at a factual or scientific level that the world was fine and that people did not have anything meaningfully called free will in any objective sense, they turned their exquisite minds to the search for meaning. The First Century had two basic responses to this search for meaning. The first was Epicureanism, the search for sensation and experience. However, this had often degenerated into a base hedonism, as the Greek world found itself politically irrelevant.

The second place, a fairly Roman contribution, is to find meaning in the duties largely fixed by your birth. While this was not yet fully-fledged Stoicism during the time Paul was writing, it's very much in the vein that would later produce Stoicism. So, the Roman world preached that your value, identity, and meaning in life could be found by doing your duty, particularly to your family. They argued that the gods themselves chose or predetermined where you would be born, and therefore, you could find meaning in doing your duty, whether as a son or a slave of a particular house.

It is this idea that Paul is riffing on in Ephesians 1. You have been spiritually reborn into a new family, and this rebirth was predestined, giving you new rights and responsibilities. You have been discovered as the heir of a family. That family is noble, royal even. How noble? It is the direct lineage of that great father "from whom every family in heaven and earth derives its name." We have joined the progenitor family, which is to say, the noblest family conceivable.

The idea is not to replace the blood family. There will always be a special bond between those who grew up around the same table, eating the same food, and submitting to the same earthly Father. But the idea is that your submission to your heavenly Father should be so complete, authentic, and all-encompassing that you can play well in the sandbox with your spiritual family. God's complete Household is part of Christ's hope in Mark 10 after the Rich Young Ruler departs.

Jesus said, "Truly, I say to you, there is no one who has left house or brothers or sisters or mother or Father or children or lands, for my sake and for the gospel, who will not receive a hundredfold now in this time, houses and brothers and sisters and mothers and children and lands, with persecutions, and in the age to come eternal life. But many who are first will be last, and the last first."

## Concluding thought:

Take one giant step back to properly view the Church as it should be and not miss our responsibility to Christ because we follow a tradition. Ask yourself how the next generation will fare from what we make the Church be during our age. Will our children receive the idea of a Church family, or will they receive a Church hierarchy? Will the coming Church cut out a piece of land they claim for Christ, or will they talk about the land God gave and then took away from Israel? Will there be far more said than done?

# Chapter 9

# THE WISE MASTER BUILDER
## Building with the Correct Materials

When writing to the Church at Corinth, the Apostle Paul began this way (I will summarize, emphasizing the main points of his opening remarks). "Paul, called as an apostle of Jesus Christ ...To the church of God which is at Corinth, to those who have been sanctified in Christ Jesus, saints by calling ...I thank my God always concerning you for the grace of God which was given you in Christ Jesus, that in everything you were enriched in Him, in all speech and all knowledge ...so that you are not lacking in any gift ...Now I exhort you, brethren, by the name of our Lord Jesus Christ, that you all agree and that there be no divisions among you, but that you be made complete in the same mind and in the same judgment." (Vs. 1-10)

Paul's opening remarks praise God for His grace on behalf of the Corinthians. He is not honoring the Corinthians, but God. God sanctified (set them apart) for His purposes. Apart from God's call, their service would have no value. God's grace enriched the Church in Christ, who gave them knowledge and gifts not previously received. They lacked nothing. In short, in a few words, Paul laid a foundation upon which the Church at Corinth will be held responsible for their service.

The rest of the letter contains misbehaviors on their part. The first act and attitude of disobedience mentioned is the one upon which all others exist; "...that you all agree and that there be no divisions among you...". People do not hurt people they actively love in loyalty, not empty sentimentality. Yet, on every page of this loving letter of Paul's, we see the sins of one Church member against another.

Denominations, sects, schisms, isms, interpretations, and historical foundations divide the Church. I am confident that division represents the Church today and for centuries. To be a faithful follower of Jesus Christ is not enough to be one with any local congregation; you must be one with the Church universal.

There is always room for non-essential differences between Churches that do not involve Biblical teaching. Biblically, according to Scripture, God does not approve of divisions of any kind. People endorse and applaud the things that make them distinct from other communities. Is being a Christian about being unique or part of the whole? Should Churches today feel guiltless about Paul's admonition, "...being diligent to preserve the unity of the Spirit in the bond of peace. here is one body and one Spirit, just as also you were called in one hope of your calling; 5one Lord, one faith, one baptism, 6one God and Father of all who is over all and through all and in all." (Ephesians 4:3-6). If church leaders and members are apathetic, they do not possess the will or the humility to correct their errors.

Is the Church universally called to unity or only the local congregation? To answer this question, I will give you the Bible. God is not confused, and neither are His writings. Every Scriptural text has multiple applications but only one interpretation. The reason for divisions in the Church is pride and not differing interpretations.

The reason for many interpretations is a refusal to interpret the Scriptures according to God's meaning rather than their biases, prejudices, and denominations. They do not trust God by allowing His word to say what He means; instead, they replace God's intent with their own. In every division, one person is correct, and everyone else that differs is wrong. The truth is narrow. Jesus is the way; there is no other way, period and narrow!

Is the sin of immorality acceptable in the Church? If not, is immortality worse than division? How vital are Jesus' words? "By this, all people will know that you are My disciples: if you have love for one another." (John 13:35). Divided people do not exemplify love. There is no better quality to demonstrate love than unity.

My dear readers, permit me to break into this train of thought to say I do not delight in criticizing the Church for divisions. If I could meet myself fifty-three years ago, I would give my other self one good talking to. You can believe me. Any kind of sin is hard to talk about because my guilt reaches the heavens after fifty-three years of knowing Christ. Therefore, I must write these things in tears because Jesus deserves better than my life.

As the Church of the suffering Son of God, we must demonstrate our love to Him by laying aside all intellectual pride and the higher learning that fuels it. As sinners who have received extravagant grace from God that brought us into the divine family, made us brethren, redeemed, forgiven, and cleansed us from all sin, we are responsible for humbling ourselves.

Let us consider some of Paul's warnings preceding 1 Corinthians 3.

"Now I urge you ...that there be no divisions among you, but that you be made complete in the same mind and in the same judgment." A little wiggle room at Paul's urging. The Greek urging is to call out and beseech us with an argument that can stand out in court.

"Has Christ been divided?" Paul gave us a blistering test of Christ's division in the following phrase - "Paul was not crucified for you, was he?" What can a pastor, preacher, Seminary professor, or elder say he was? If not, I suggest we back off and let God's word say what it means.

"I will destroy the wisdom of the wise..." Human wisdom gets in the way; all divisions spring from human understanding. Therefore, let us replace human pride with spiritual knowledge and eliminate divisions. "Has God not made foolish the wisdom of the world?" Why would any man of God want to partake in a knowledge that would make him foolish? The fool has said in his heart there is no God." (Psalm 14:1). Let the Church hear; the world's wisdom is for fools and is present in every doctrinal error.

"God has chosen the foolish things of the world to shame the wise…" God has not chosen many to be equal in this way. Why on earth does the Church feel it necessary to compete with the learning of the world? I would only count on it if, of course, Paul got it wrong.

"Due to Him (God) that you are in Christ Jesus, who became to us wisdom from God…" All authentically wise men agree and are in Christ Jesus. Everyone who accepts foolish teaching and is content to do so is also satisfied to be outside Christ.

"Let the one who boasts boast in the LORD." The inference is that in the Church at Corinth, people were boasting. Let us remember the context is one of division and intellectual pride that resulted in human reasoning. Can we say pride doesn't exist in us today? Are we content to remain in such a place, or are we crying out to God for revival?

It is necessary to divide the Church into two basic camps, lest each group point its finger at the other and avoid conviction of sin. Each group may be weaker differently, but the tempter is shrewd enough to defeat a person either way. Some people depend more upon intellect; others rely more upon emotions.

Pride is not a stranger to either camp; it merely has arrived differently.

"I did not come as someone superior in speaking ability..." Some teachers, like their sermons, are dry as dust despite their intellectual prowess.

"but in demonstration of the Spirit and of power..." Some preachers are highly emotional, which confuses the Spirit's power. The measure of power is neither intellect nor feelings but the obedience that fuels worship pleasing to God. The Church's highest standard of compliance is unity. God is three in one. The man was made and always meant to be in the image of God. There is no division with the Godhead. Any division with the body of Christ is a blow to God's image. The great sin of unbelief says, "I can't change the church all over the world." You don't have to, but you should allow God by the resurrection of Christ from the dead to change you.

"But we have the mind of Christ." Let not the reader say, "I preach the Gospel, and I am not a natural man, and because I understand the Gospel, I am spiritual." Paul wrote to the Church at Corinth, and as such, he recognized the gifts given to them, "And God has appointed in the Church, first apostles, second prophets, third teachers..." They preached the Gospel, which did not excuse them for their pride and divisiveness.

# Mere Men and Godly Men Exposed

The preceding foundation brings us to the Wise Master Builder of Chapter 3.

Mere Men And Godly Men Exposed

"So then neither the one who plants nor the one who waters is anything, but God who causes the growth." (1 Corinthians 3;7)

In the above verse, the Apostle says man is nothing. God causes all things, and apart from God, man cannot make anything even grow. Therefore, God is the source of all good things! It is a simple message and magnificently profound. "Every good thing given and every perfect gift is from above, coming down from the Father of lights…" (James 1:17)

Two-thirds of the angelic host has consistently lived out the reality of God's centricity to all created things since the day they began. One-third of the hosts broke from the light of God's importance and became a god in their own hearts.

In the Garden of Eden, the entire human race under Adam and Eve's headship, our first parents, followed Satan in self-worship. Therefore, deception has captured our hearts, and our reasonings place value upon ourselves that is not reality. The word Church in Greek is ekklésia: an assembly, congregation, the whole body of Christian believers whom God calls out from the world and into His eternal kingdom.

We expect the world to live under the lies of self and

demonic deception, even young believers, but to a mature Church belongs the truth. However, the Church at Corinth was gifted and blessed abundantly by God's grace, yet remained immature. Furthermore, they were not only immature, but the source of their behavior was the flesh.

"And I, brethren, could not speak to you as to spiritual men, but as to men of flesh, as to infants in Christ. I gave you milk to drink, not solid food; for you were not yet able to receive it. Indeed, even now you are not yet able, for you are still fleshly. For since there is jealousy and strife among you, are you not fleshly, and are you not walking like mere men? For when one says, "I am of Paul," and another, "I am of Apollos," are you not mere men?" (1 Corinthians 3:1-4)

Believe it or not, the Church is called to be a people of more than mere men; it is called to be men invested with the Spirit of the living God. People are not called to self-exaltation of their spirituality when, in fact, they are nothing more than emotional. A reality that goes unnoticed when they continue in the flesh and not in the Spirit.

Dead orthodoxy parading as doctrinally sound is dead because of intellectual pride, and dead worship parading as emotional worshipers is dead because of sensual satisfaction.

The light of the Gospel has not reached them in their heart. It has not rescued them from jealousy, strife, and a list carried through every chapter in the entire letter. Paul's conclusion was the immature and carnal state the Church never grew beyond.

"And I, brethren, could not speak to you as to spiritual men, but as to men of flesh, as to infants in Christ. I gave you milk to drink, not solid food; for you were not yet able to receive it. Indeed, even now you are not yet able, for you are still fleshly." (1 Corinthians 3:1, 2)

Every Church leader and member reading these scriptures should be cautious not to assume their Church is in a better condition than Corinth. Any Christian congregation that is not broken over the divided nature of the Church worldwide and is not spending much time on its knees to pray for unity is not spiritually minded. Those who take sinful behavior as just the way things have to be, and there is nothing we can do about it cannot care about the sufferings of Christ the way they should.

## Fleshly and Spiritual Men Explained

In Chapter Three, Paul identified the Corinthian problem as living according to the flesh and not the Spirit. "And I, brethren, could not speak to you as to spiritual men, but as to men of flesh" (1 Corinthians 3:1). The explanation of what Paul meant is explained in Romans 8:5. "For those who are according to the flesh set their minds on the things of the flesh, but those who are according to the Spirit, the things of the Spirit."

According to Greek (katá), "down from a higher to a lower plane, with special reference to the end-point." It is a direction taken in mind. So those who are according to the flesh begin by focusing on the body's needs. Since the focus is down, the only way a person can go from the body is down into unrestrained lust. In the end, such a person will sin willfully.

Paul uses two phrases in Romans: the one we just explained and the second. "Set their minds" is (phronéō) from phrḗn, the diaphragm, the parts around the heart. Phronéō essentially equates to personal opinion fleshing itself out in action (J. Thayer). It regulates from within, as inner perspective (insight) shows itself by corresponding outward behavior.

Therefore, the person setting their mind on the Spirit begins by thinking about life at its highest level. They think about God, His will, purposes, and plans. God's will becomes most pertinent to how they live it out as they suppose downward. This thinking, perspective, and corresponding behavior is a life lived on the highest plane.

Another phrase used by Paul is "On the flesh" is sárks ("flesh") in Greek. It is not always evil in Scripture. Indeed, it is positive with sexual intercourse in marriage (Eph 5:31) and for the sinless human body of Jesus (Jn 1:14; 1 Jn 4:2,3). Indeed, flesh (what is physical) is necessary for the body to live out the faith the Lord works in (Gal 2:20).]

However, sarcasm is generally negative, referring to making decisions (actions) according to self. Activities apart from faith and independent from God's inworking is sin. "But he who doubts is condemned if he eats because his eating is not from faith; and whatever is not from faith is sin" (Romans 14:23).

Therefore, what is "of the flesh (carnal)" is, by definition, displeasing to the Lord – even things that seem "respectable!" In short, flesh generally relates to unaided human effort, decisions (actions) that originate from self or are empowered by self. Carnality "of the flesh" proceeds from the unchanged part of us. Whatever is not transformed by God.

## Judgment of The Privileged

With the terms according to the flesh and set their minds on the Spirit fixed in our minds, let us consider the tragic and glorious results of two ways of living in contrast.

According to Paul, there is evidence by which to judge our present behavior. In his words, "For since there is jealousy and strife among you, are you not fleshly?" His words are clear; therefore, our present condition should be equally apparent. If the local Church assembly is content to be at odds with other communities, are we spiritual or carnal? If we say, what can I do to change things and become complacent, are we carnal or spiritual?

Let us add another wrinkle. Paul wrote, "What then is Apollos? And what is Paul? Servants through whom you believed." He magnifies servanthood and denigrates praising men. His following phrase proves my point. "...even as the Lord gave opportunity to each one." The Lord gave opportunity; the servant can become a tool through whom the Lord works or not. Either way, the tool is just an agency. There is a reward for the servant if he sets his mind on the Spirit. The congregation is required to regard the preacher as an agent of God, even as the pastor should.

Therefore, Paul restates his point. "So then neither the one who plants nor the one who waters is anything." There's no escaping it; man is nothing apart from God. We become idolatrous if we view men in such a way as to make them more than they are. When we avoid idolatry, we exalt God. "But God who causes the growth." Does God get all the glory, or what part does the pastor receive?

If you say you are exalting God and not idolizing men, Paul's following phrase will be entirely relevant for you, and if it is not valid in actuality, it will bother you. "Now he who plants and he who waters are one." What makes God's servants one is accurate and relevant humility, nothing else. To sidestep and rationalize the humility that makes men be men and God to be God is nothing if it does not produce a change in our thinking and behavior.

If we disagree on theology across denominational lines, we cannot be content until we agree. Prayer and fasting can change us unless we believe God cannot. Where is the faith in such thinking?

Perhaps the problem is that we don't want to change. Now, that's a problem because judgment is coming! Paul laid a foundation, and on it, the building continued. The Scriptures are still used to proclaim the Gospel of Jesus Christ. They have not changed, but neither have the problems within the Church. A warning was declared to Corinth, which is reported today if you follow Jesus Christ. "But each man must be careful how he builds on it."

Be careful is the term blépō, which means to observe something physical with spiritual results. A spiritual man's perception is understanding the non-physical and immaterial realm resulting from looking at something material. Developing a spiritual man's insight is taking action and responding correctly.

Good responses will save us from the fire that will test our work. "Now if any man builds on the foundation with gold, silver, precious stones, wood, hay, straw, each man's work will become evident; for the day will show it because it is to be revealed with fire, and the fire itself will test the quality of each man's work." (Vs.12, 13)

Of course, gold, silver, and precious stones cannot be burned. Nevertheless, they are purified by fire. They are the things that will last. Wood, hay, and stubble will not withstand the fire but will be lost. Sin is never the issue in this judgment because Christ already paid the price for all sin through His sufferings. God will never entertain sin, where His Son was offered as a sacrifice. Therefore, we read in 2 Corinthians 5:10. "For we must all appear before the judgment seat of Christ, so that each one may be recompensed for his deeds in the body, according to what he has done, whether good or bad."

The word bad in Greek is phaulos, which means something ordinary, worthless, of no account. It is akin to the German word foul, which smells terrible because it has become useless. The life of obedience to God is a life of faith, whereby human effort becomes a stench to the believer himself. Few start this way, but we learn to discern between good and worthless works in time and sanctifying chastisement.

God's ways are not our ways, and for this reason, we can be wrong even when we seek to do good things for the kingdom of God. Some things are hard to hear because they go against what seems right in our eyes. "There is a way which seems right to a man, but its end is the way of death" (Proverbs 14:12). How much heartache would we save ourselves if we would accept the proverb as accurate when we are convinced our way is right, even though it stands against God's ways.

## The Fire of Testing

Paul continued, "If anyone's work which he has built on it remains, he will receive a reward" (Vs. 14). How we think about rewards at this point is crucial because it will motivate us to do the Lord's best or make us numb and useless to God. If our focus is on some earthly reward, a thing, or a position, it will be lost. If we seek a prize that cannot fade away by God's grace, we will receive it throughout eternity.

The best way to see life is through our Lord's eyes. How and why we live our lives is the all-important question to answer. For this answer, we will look to the author of Hebrews, who quotes and expounds Psalm 40:7. "Sacrifices and offerings and whole burnt offerings and offerings for sin you have not desired, nor have you taken pleasure in them" (Which are offered according to the Law). He said, "Behold, I have come to do your will. He takes away the first in order to establish the second." God built the Old Testament system upon a covenant that required man's obedience. In that system, men continually sinned and continuously needed the offering of blood on their behalf. The priest offered the sacrifice of bulls and goats. Unfortunately, the blood of bulls and goats is worthless in removing sin. It only pointed to a better and perfect covenant between God, the Father, and His beloved Son.

Many vital matters become apparent through the two covenants: one, man's inability to please God; two, only God can please God; three, and most importantly, God the Father's willingness to love God the Son and men entirely, and in that order.

"Nor have I taken pleasure in them." There was never pleasure in the Old Testament sacrifices. The priests were sinners, and the blood was from animals. Even if the blood had been from men, it would not satisfy because all men are sinful. God would never sacrifice men made in His image. God values all life; the animal kingdom came under man's dominion, and they have paid a terrible price for our sins (Romans, 8).

"Behold, I have come to do your will." The beloved Son, Jesus Christ, our Lord, left His place in the Divine Trinity and became a man. Jesus gave more than we can imagine, fulfilling His Father's will. What is important to Jesus Christ is God the Father. His purpose needs to become our purpose.

When we die to our selfish pride and fleshly lusts, then the will of God becomes our motivating purpose for life. When the sufferings of Christ motivate us, then His dying words will have meaning and give us purpose that pleases the Father. "The glory which You have given Me I also have given to them, so that they may be one, just as We are one; I in them and You in Me, that they may be perfected in unity, so that the world may know that You sent Me" (John 17:22, 23).

We know Jesus' intentions from His dying words on the road to Gethsemane. The only question we need to answer honestly is, do we care? Do we care enough to die to see them fulfilled?

The last part of the quote from Hebrews 10 explains what has been written. "He takes away the first to establish the second." The first was according to the Law. A law that, at best, was obeyed out of obligation, else, or broken. God replaced it with obedience with the best motive of love and self-sacrificial behavior.

The first and best reward for the obedient and spiritual Son will be having pleased the Son with His sacrificial love. If that is not the case, consider the alternative. You are standing before Christ and seeing your works turn into cinders in the fire of

God's judgment. "If anyone's work is burned up, he will suffer loss; but he himself will be saved, yet only so as through fire" (Vs. 15). How do you think that will make you feel?

When, with an enlarged mind, we consider the sufferings of Christ and begin to realize just how much He suffered on our behalf, only God will be able to wipe away our tears.

## The Fruit of Love

Paul concludes chapter 3 in verses 18 to 23 by returning his argument against highly exalting men to a place we do not belong. Verse 21 is boxed in between Paul's warnings to avoid the foolish thinking of the world and the exultation of Christ and God to whom all things belong. Verse 21 is centrally placed as the key to his main point. "So then, no one is to be boasting in people."

Boasting in people is destructive to the Church. The Church is a people called out of the world to house the person of the living God. The world is foreign to God, and it hates Him. The foolishness of which Paul speaks in 18 to 20 is self-exaltation. The world makes statues of great men to praise them as if God did not exist. The world's thinking is destructive to the Church.

When Paul talks about the fire of God's judgment that will fall upon His elect, he then speaks about destroying God's temple. "Do you not know that you are a temple of God and that the Spirit of God dwells in you? If any man destroys the temple of God, God will destroy him, for the temple of God is holy, and that is what you are.' (Vs. 16, 17)

The word destroy in our English translation, phtheírō, is from phthiō, "perish or waste away." It means to destroy because it is a corrupting influence that causes a thing to deteriorate. In this context, the corrupting influence is the preoccupation with man's importance and centrality to the Church. In reality, God is central to the Church, and there is nothing else.

Those who take the Church's attention off of Christ and place it upon the importance of men corrupt the temple of God. For nine hundred years, the Church placed all attention upon itself to the exclusion of the Gospel. At the Reformation, God recovered the Gospel from the false Church, but men did not repent from their preoccupation with themselves. To this day, we continue to corrupt God's institution by wrongfully exalting our leaders.

Some may argue that when it says, "God will destroy him," does that mean God will corrupt his children? God chastens his children to bring forth the peaceable fruit of righteousness, Hebrews 12. The parable of the sower in Mark 4 contains three deficient soils and one good. Concerning the good soil, Jesus said, "And those are the ones sown with seed on the good soil; and they hear the word and accept it and bear fruit, thirty, sixty, and a hundred times as much." Please note that all good soil does not bear the same amount of fruit.

Regarding Pharaoh, the Scripture says he hardened his

heart; also, Pharaoh's heart was hardened, and God hardened Pharaoh's heart. God is light, which means He tells the truth, and like the sun, God's light has different effects. The same sun that softens the wax hardens the clay.

God's children possess a transformed heart so that it will produce thirty times the fruit at the very least. God gives His children the indwelling Spirit to convict us of sin. He has provided His precious word to show us the light of truth so we may discern right from wrong and good from evil. However, if we do not listen, we will face the fire of His judgment at the Bema seat of Christ. If the saint's work burns up, he will suffer loss but be saved through the fire.

If we are not purified on this side of heaven, we surely will be on the other. We will become what God wants us to be.

In times past, revival transformed sinful people into a unified body of saints that proclaimed the Gospel without compromise or division. The first occurrence was at Pentecost, where we read. "Day by day continuing with one mind in the temple, and breaking bread from house to house; they were taking their meals together with gladness and sincerity of heart, praising God and having favor with all the people." (Acts 2:46, 47).

Please take special note that they continued with one mind and had favor with all the people. Furthermore, as Jesus enjoyed popularity for a time, the Church received the same because of its love. The world will always turn upon the people of God.

In the eighteenth century, a revival rivaled Pentecost.; it was called The Great Awakening. As a result of God pouring out His Spirit upon this land for thirty years, tens of thousands of sinners joined the ranks of the saints. Their testimony was graven so profoundly in the hearts of the culture that America was born.

The United States has stood for just that unity. People from different nations, religions, and cultures worldwide have come to this land to become one people. Please consider that God has turned a pagan country into a beacon of freedom and unity.

Another day is coming when Christ will set up another earthly rule for one thousand years. During that time, Christ will reign with His people and continually pour out His Spirit to the saving multitudes will be added to the ranks of the redeemed. Jesus will pour out more light on a rejuvenated earth than ever before.

Finally, Satan will be released once again to deceive the nations. Blood will be spilled where he reigns. Except in that hour, the only blood spilled will belong to sinners. Then comes the final judgment.

The Church should always pray for revival because it is always in need.

# Chapter 10

## UNLESS A SEED FALLS TO THE GROUND
### The Christian Understanding of Victory

God's people do not take possession of any land as a loving community of obedient followers of Jesus Christ to be successful and live abundant lives for selfish reasons. However, often in history, when and wherever Christians were permitted to live without persecution, they succeeded in being plentiful.

There are always two elements involved in living for Christ. The first is abundant living rightfully defined, which is godly character, separation from the world's ways, and a self-sacrificing approach to life. The second is motivation. Christianity results from people moved by the hand of God to take God's holy Word seriously, practically, and often at the cost of their lives. Therefore, we need to answer the question: why live a godly life?

When Christianity is authentic, the answer to why Christians live as they do is always the same - out of obedience to Jesus

Christ, who gave His life so they might have eternal life. The love at Christ's cross is why Christians are obedient to God.

This chapter will briefly examine the prophetic nature of God's Holy Word, the power and effects of authentic salvation in a believer's life, and how the church should treat prophetic passages that are yet future.

# Eschatology: Its Method and Motivation

## The Method

Eschatology is the prophetic nature of God's Word. The Bible is far more than another book; it proves to be authentic, supernatural, transcendent, and divine by its prophetic nature. Prophecy is the method God has used to verify the authenticity of His Word because it is miraculous and impossible by human means.

Divine prophecy is in two tenses; the first is fulfillment in the past. It must be understood through proper study and means of interpretation; the second, yet future, must be received by faith. Faith is never blind but built upon reasonable and verifiable elements in the text studied.

A perfect example of proper interpretation is the book by J. Warner Wallace, Cold-Case Christianity. Within its pages are many efficient means of understanding the verifiable ways divine prophecy is understood. A cold-case L.A. detective for twenty years, Wallace effectively understood how to open cold cases and, by comparing the testimonies of eyewitnesses plus circumstantial evidence, concluded whether they were telling the truth.

As an atheist, Wallace decided to disprove the Bible, but in the process, he had to conclude it was accurate and truthful, and by doing so, he became a Christian. Space only allows for one example. The four Gospels contain not just four but many eyewitness accounts of the historical facts that occurred. He proves that they were not contrived but verifiably authentic. Wallace concluded by scientific and logical means in his book the authenticity revealed in the Bible.

## The Motivation

"Then I fell at his feet to worship him. But he said to me, "Do not do that; I am a fellow servant of yours and your brethren who hold the testimony of Jesus; worship God. For the testimony of Jesus is the spirit of prophecy." (Revelation 19:10)

People believe when they become aware that the Bible is not just another book but is divinely inspired and powerful to change their lives. The Bible is reasonable and verifiable, as I discussed above. However, another element in believing still exists the presence of the Holy Spirit of God. Considering communication through the Holy Spirit, Romans 8:16 tells us, "The Spirit Himself testifies with our spirit that we are children of God." Such a spiritual connection is vitally necessary for believing and understanding that God is real, living, and willing to communicate with those He saves.

Furthermore, the viability of past and proven prophecies makes the reality of predictions yet to come all the more powerful. In Revelation 19:10 above, John, by hearing from Jesus Christ directly while still imperfect and in His presence, and the holy angels became overwhelmed. In his condition, he bowed to worship an angel and was reproved for him. "Do not do that," the angel said. Then comes the revealing statement, "The testimony of Jesus is the spirit of prophecy."

Spirit in Greek is (*pneúma)* and means *spirit* or Holy *Spirit, wind,* or *breath.* The most frequent meaning in the New Testament is "*spirit.*" Only the context, however, determines which sense is meant. From this statement by the angel, we are charged to look at the divine authorship of the Bible. Just as God breathed into Adam, the first man, even so, He breathed into the Bible His life, by which the book of words is alive and powerful.

"For the word of God is living and active and sharper than any two-edged sword, and piercing as far as the division of soul and spirit, of both joints and marrow and able to judge the thoughts and intentions of the heart." (Hebrews 4:12) Therefore, the angel tells us that prophecy, past, and future are God's very life and power.

The motivation to live our lives for God is God. All people are responsible for living for God because no one would exist without His creative act, even in procreation. The Bible, God's Word, takes our responsibility to another level. Within its pages are not just verifiable events of the past that speak of God's hand in everything that takes place but also His loving work to save.

In prophecies from the Old Testament, as in Isaiah 52 and 53, we can read of Christ's coming hundreds of years before God became a man in the person of His obedient Son to become a sacrificial offering for sin's penalty and retribution. When placed upon a sinful man, this penalty takes an eternity that Jesus Christ endured in every saved sinner's place: these and many more motivations are for living a godly and obedient life.

## Eternal Life: Its Power and Effect

### The Power

In America, we live in one of the most successful, productive, and free societies the world has ever known. Even a brief history review reveals the cause and nature of our success and freedom. The principles upon which our nation is based are undeniably Christian. Throughout our history, the principles have been present, but that is not to say there has always been the reality and presence of the living God in people's lives.

The presence of God is always, and in every case, reformative. Where the Holy Spirit is, there is the transformation from sinner to saint. Saint, as defined by, called to live unto

God and not for selfish reasons. Therefore, the fact needs to be understood, as Jesus said in Matthew 7:21, "Not everyone who says to Me, 'Lord, Lord,' will enter the kingdom of heaven, but the one who does the will of My Father who is in heaven *will enter*."

The foundation of America was undeniably the Bible. Still, not everyone living in America was Christian, not even the nation's fathers, who sat under the teaching of passionate preaching during what was known as The Great Awakening. After thirty-four years of hell, fire, and brimstone preaching, with an offer of unfathomable grace and love at the cross of Christ invitations, many knew only the sermons and the Lord's name. The principles of Christianity without the presence or power of God in individual lives will eventually erode even the way of life, not to mention the religion that is useless to a godless generation.

There is still, at present, religion in America. Nevertheless, in considerable measure, it is compromised by evil motives, the absence of the Holy Spirit of God in many churches, and an unwillingness to live by God's Word, even though it is preached every Sunday morning, to one degree or another. Christianity is only present when God is present. God is present when His Word is heard and obeyed.

At this point, it is vitally important that we underscore the reason for obedience. There are principles that, when applied, can reap successful results; however, they are tainted by selfish motives and not out of love for God. In Isaiah 58, there is the witness of God against His people, that is, His people in name only. They go through all the religious rituals, but their heart is for evil, and God despises their empty religion. As in Jesus' words above, they call Him "Lord, Lord," but they shall not enter the kingdom of heaven. Why? The kingdom of God they were building on earth was a reproach to the name of God because it was done with evil intent for selfish reasons, and it was in God's name only and not because they loved and obeyed Him. They were living ungodly and worse than the people of the land that God punished when He gave it to them.

In contrast to Israel and America referred to above, there are authentic success stories of God's Word in the lives of communities and people throughout history that tell a very different story. As one example, there are the missionary endeavors of the nineteenth century. When travel was still arduous and limiting, scores of people left their homelands and ventured to other cultures and people groups, giving their lives away to God and them, as it were, for a higher and eternal purpose.

There was William Carey in the backdrop of impoverished India for many years without even seeing a single convert but continued waiting for God's blessing, maybe in this life but certainly in the next. There was Hudson Taylor, who left his motherland to reach the multitudes of China. It might not be considered multitudes by today's standards, but it certainly was then. He spent his time as a doctor in missionary work, prayed in the wee hours of the morning, gave himself wholeheartedly to work, and lost a dear child in the process.

Building a community has always been challenging, and even Hudson wrote of the hardship of others following him to China to help and became more of a burden. That is not to say that all who followed him were a burden. There are God's people who never rise as they might because they allow the ways of the world, their sinful flesh, or the devil to do them so much harm that they become useless in God's plan for taking over a plot of land for His cause.

Both men were native to England when the sun never set on the British Aisles. They sacrificed the pleasures of this life for a season to please and obey God and gain an eternal reward. Their lives and hundreds, if not thousands of others, followed God's plan to be a beacon of light to a condemned and dying world.

## The Effect

The effect of eternal life is twofold. First, there is a power for godly living for those who,

by God's grace, believe God's Word and receive the infusion of God's life. His life is not biological, which is created, but it is timeless; it is union with God Himself so that the person can partake of God's characteristics, will, and being. This communion is what we call transformation. It is the separation from the world, its ways and philosophies, and separation to the obedience and honor due to God the creator. Such separation God calls sanctification.

The second effect of eternal life is the world's reaction to those who have been sanctified. There is jealousy on the one side for not having what they see in others, and that jealousy can be good or evil. Evil jealousy usually brings resentment, animosity, anger, and even persecution. Good jealousy helps bring sinners to repentance and faith because of the changed lives they witness and the community that forms around them if done according to God's Word.

Christianity began on the Day of Pentecost when Peter preached the first sermon to the people of Israel who were present when Christ was crucified. Israel was meant to be a light to the surrounding nations, but they failed because, in their unrepentant condition, they never believed God's message that they were unacceptable and evil under the law. However, as the Holy Spirit moved among the people in those days, they repented of their sins, turned to God's faithfulness to His prophetic Word, and sent His Son, whom they beheld and received, but not all of them. There has always been only a remnant of people who believe.

There were revivals throughout Israel's history. As in the case of Ezra when the people returned from their seventy-year captivity. Some think that the longest of the Psalms, Psalm one-hundred and nineteen, was written by Ezra. Why? Because he was a man of the Word. When others became unfaithful, even at that time, he remained faithful because he wanted to honor God by obeying His Holy Word.

The nation was unfaithful because they twisted God's Word and thought they could be good by keeping God's Word when, in reality, the scriptures were as a schoolmaster to bring the people to Christ for salvation by being condemned by the law. Only sinners need to repent, and all people are sinners. Therefore, the power of God has always been seen in transforming a life. Like Nehemiah and all the prophets, Ezra was a transformed man who experienced harsh treatment, rejection, and some even death at the hands of their countrymen. They called sin sin and would not say what the people wanted to hear. In the lives of transformed people, we see the power of God to save. When God saves a person, He also gives them the willingness to hear what He says and the ability to understand it. God is the author of His Word and must also be the One to give its meaning.

However, the power to transform a person is only part of God's work in the world. Noah was a preacher of righteousness for one hundred and twenty years before God destroyed the world by a worldwide flood. Concerning his life and testimony, we read in Hebrews 11:7, "By faith Noah, being warned *by God* about things not yet seen, in reverence prepared an ark for the salvation of his household, by which he condemned the world, and became an heir of the righteousness which is according to faith."

**Let us notice some aspects of Noah's life from verse seven:**

1. Noah lived by faith.
2. The verse tells us that his faith was not blind because God warned him. At certain times, rare as they have been, God talked to people to convey His will.
3. Even though God spoke to Noah, the things God said would come to pass as yet were unseen to him.
4. Noah acted out of reverence for God. Something which sinners born to Adam's race are unwilling and unable to do, but Noah did. (Romans 8:7)
5. Noah prepared an ark to float on water in a world that was without water as we now know it. It didn't ever rain in the days of Noah. We can't imagine the kind of razzing and ridicule that Noah would have faced from such a violent and hateful world as the pre-flood one. Still, he finished the ark.
6. The scriptures tell us that Noah saved his household. The term household is essential in our study because we need to think beyond individual families to the households of the church. It begins with the family unit according to the flesh in Noah's case. Still, salvation extends the family to all believers who, by their community, make the world jealous, enlightened, and, unfortunately, condemned if they don't change.
7. Noah, by his reverence for God, by adhering to the Word spoken to him and not rejecting it as the rest of

the world did, and saving his household, condemned the rest of the world. He did not judge the world or condemn them in his heart as if he were better than them, but his actions did. In Peter's second letter, 2:5, he spoke of God's saving Noah and call to preach "but preserved Noah, a preacher of righteousness." Noah was a saved sinner who began living the right way for God.

8. By Noah's actions, he became an heir of the righteousness by faith. An heir receives something by a birthright. He doesn't earn it or work for it. Noah's righteousness was bequeathed to him. Therefore, since he received righteousness as an heir by God's grace, his faith was also received as an heir. The transforming work of God is all of God. Noah building the ark and preaching under persecution was possible as a gift of salvation.

As quoted in this chapter, "Not everyone who says to Me, 'Lord, Lord,' will enter the kingdom of heaven, **but the one who does the will of My Father** who is in heaven *will enter.*" (Matthew 7:21). The person who claims salvation or being a Christian is not saved if a changed heart and life do not accompany their words. As stated in this chapter, such transformation is never perfect, and people can be sidetracked. However, there is little to no biblical accountability as commanded in many places in the New Testament, such as Matthew 18, in most churches in America.

I doubt that many pastors even have the discernment, due to lack of use, to discern the appearance of salvation versus an unsaved but religious person. The effect of eternal life in a person's heart is a new way of looking at life, changed actions that follow, and love and devotion to the Word of God.

# Eschatology: as Forth and Foretelling

## As Forth-telling

We need not spend much time on this topic because we have already entertained in some detail that the Word of God changes lives. Nevertheless, it is vitally important that all of God's Word is prophetic because it comes from God. Apart from God's special revelation, man cannot understand God or His ways. Therefore, all scripture is prophetic in bringing forth things unknown to the spiritually dead human race. Paul states the above principle perfectly when he wrote to the Corinthian church 14:1 and 3, "Pursue love, yet earnestly desire spiritual *gifts,* but especially that you may prophesy." Paul's use of "prophesy" in verse 1 does not tell of future things because he defined it in verse 3. "But the one who prophesies speaks to people *for* edification, exhortation, and consolation." Therefore, Paul uses the word prophesy to build people up, give them a stern warning, and console them in their troubles.

We must be clear about the Word prophecy as if it only

meant the telling of future events. To prophesy in 1 Corinthians 14:31 is used as instructive. "For you can all **prophesy** in turn so that everyone may be instructed and encouraged." A prophetic word can be encouraging by telling a future, even like the return of Christ, or it can be encouraging by instruction. Understanding what it means to identify with Christ or be filled with the Holy Spirit is encouraging instruction, but there is nothing future about them.

**Forth-telling** may be defined as speaking forth out of God's written Word. Sunday mornings in a good church, the scriptures are expounded upon, explaining their meaning and in the context of helpful information for godly living. There can be no holy living that pleases God apart from understanding and applying His holy Word, the Bible.

## As Foretelling

From the beginning, the devil was a liar, and till today, he and demons still work very hard to confuse God's Word and work by filling it with lies. There can be no more significant weapon against demonic intrusion in the church than the truth. The Bible is truth. At the point of prophecy as foretelling, the devil goes into overdrive. Why? Because prophecy of the future return of Jesus Christ is an excellent ally in the fight against moral impurity, but the impurity of compromise is the most destructive weapon forged against God's people. The great sin of Israel for twelve hundred years was compromise. It is all over their history. They were choosing the idols of the land, to have a king, all the way to burning their babies in the fire to appease the false gods of the surrounding nations. They were continually choosing to compromise, compromise, compromise. John tells us just how powerful the knowledge of Christ's return is, as stated in 1 John 3:2, 3, emphasis added. "We know that when He appears, we will be like Him, because we will see Him just as He is. And everyone who has this hope *set* on Him purifies himself, just as He is pure."

For an authentic believer, there can be no more incredible motivator to live a godly life than to know that one day you will be like your savior, lover of your soul, and friend. We will not be like God with all His infinite attributes, but we will be without sin and made to perfection. All the consequences of sin will come to an end, and all the flaws in our character will be done away.

"We will see Him as He is" means complete transparency, and transparency means friendship. Jesus said, "No longer do I call you slaves, for the slave does not know what his master is doing; but I have called you friends, for all things that I have heard from My Father I have made known to you." Jesus called His disciples trusted friends. You know what it means to be a trusted friend of the son of God.

It was Dwight L. Moody who told the story of two friends during the Civil War. At the time a friend was shot and dying, he gave a letter to his friend to give to his parents. After the war, things were hard for the friend who was left, but eventually, he made his way to their home. But when he arrived, he looked like the beggar he was. The parents read the letter, which said. "The man giving you the letter is Charles, my most trusted friend, he was with me at the time of my death. Please treat him as you would me." What wouldn't those parents do for such a friend to their departed son?

What God the Father does for those who trust His Son at His death is to purify them as His Son is pure. The purity of which John speaks is not just justification in the courtroom of God's judgment or the transference of Christ's righteousness for our sin's guilt. But also a purity of sanctification in the closet of the saint's prayer life. God forgives and cleanses His children who diligently and persistently seek Him.

We will conclude this chapter by considering how confused Christians may react incorrectly concerning Christ's return. The first incorrect reaction to Christ's coming is to stop working because Jesus may come at any moment, so why build a world where things end? The second way to react is to realize we don't know when He will return, and therefore, we should build a community that will change the world and be a light until He returns. We'll call those in the first category the expectant non-worldly idle; those in the second are the non-expectant worldly diligent.

# The Expectant, non-worldly idle

When considering the people in this first category, we must remember the purpose previously stated for living as believers. The purpose stated was obedience to God. Why? When Jesus was confronted by a religious leader trying to test Him, he asked what is the first great commandment? Jesus replied by quoting Deuteronomy 6:4-5.

"Hear, Israel! The LORD is our God, the LORD is one! And you shall love the LORD your God with all your heart and with all your soul and with all your strength." As stated above, there should be no confusion in the heart of a believer in Jesus Christ regarding his duty and response to the Son of God. Love causes obedience, allegiance, honor, and glory to God the Son.

The idea that we don't know when Jesus may return; therefore, let's do nothing as if that were not disobedience is entirely demonic. It is a lie of the worst kind. Jesus said, "Go into all the world and make disciples," Why? Because all authority in heaven and earth was given to Him. Only a person who does not understand authority or chooses to reject it will turn aside from building the kingdom of Christ in light of His great love for us.

Why is the church in its present state in America? Where Christians are willing to spend seventy hours a week on a job and no time learning how to disciple others and then discipling others to Christ. Because they have no vision for building the church and because what the church is, is not in clear focus either.

The church comprises households of believers whose focus in life is to build a kingdom of obedient followers of Jesus Christ. It is not showing up for an hour on a Sunday morning and thinking you've done everything necessary to please God. Showing up may please the pastor, but no person living in such a manner will hear a well done, good, and faithful servant. Such a person may enter heaven but, after passing through the fire of the Son's Bema (judgment) seat, will lose more than they thought possible (2 Corinthians 5:10).

## The Non-expectant Worldly, Diligent

The group we are lumping people into, knowing full well that people are far too individuals with varying personalities and spiritual gifts to relegate them to a group. However, suppose you are one to believe the scriptures and believe what they say, as in spiritual warfare. In that case, there are demonic beings with authority and God-given limits that, in serving the purposes of God, lead away from the faith false converts; some tempt and lead astray, to some extent, children of God.

Paul, when writing to one of his disciples and son in the faith, said, "But the Spirit explicitly says that in later times some will fall away from the faith, paying attention to deceitful spirits and doctrines of demons" (1 Timothy 4:1). One of the ways that demons work is in the creation of teachings. From where do you think evolution came?

How many Christian brothers, starting in the sixties, fell prey to that demonic lie? There have been a multitude of doctrines that have led authentic Christians astray as well as nominal. The teaching set before us is as much an internal disposition to how to live as it is a formal teaching.

In a person's mind, it sounds something like this. We don't know when Jesus will return; He has given us our marching orders; therefore, let us work until He returns. This thought can work itself out incorrectly in any number of ways. Perhaps the most subtle and dangerous is to work hard at being successful so you can say to others (The world), "Look at me, I am living for God and see what He has done." The problem arises with the word success. Earlier in the chapter, I said the problem with success is that it can be built upon Christian principles. When principles are used to exclude prayerful intimacy with God, then it is His principles at work, but God might be letting a person go their own way because of pride. Hear what James has to say.

"Therefore, whoever wishes to be a friend of the world makes himself an enemy of God. Therefore, *it* says, "God is opposed to the proud but gives grace to the humble." (James 4:5-6). It is all too easy to be deceived in pride, especially when it feels like we are giving God all the glory. There are far too many warnings about the abundance of riches, such as, "Instruct those who are rich in this present world not to be conceited or to fix their hope on the uncertainty of riches, but on God, who richly supplies us with all things to enjoy" (1 Timothy 6:17).

How many pastors fall to pride, thinking they could not be more for God than being in "the ministry." God may cause ten men to undergo severe trials, and nine will be the better for it. God may allow ten men to be successful, and one will be the better for it. No one should ever underestimate the devil's ability to build pride in a person through "success."

# The Finish

Church planting and building is the key to waiting eagerly for Christ's return or not waiting for God at all. We work to build the church because God told us to. How we build is as vital as building at all. If building a church is a concern for a building, a parking lot, numbers in attendance, the sound of the music, or dozens of unimportant matters, then the focus is not building the church of Jesus Christ.

The church is about people. Are the people participating in church worship saved? This state of people is the first question that must be answered regularly. Is instruction in discipleship understood clearly by leadership, and can they mature people? So often, much teaching is done but little to no effect. How do you know? Some will ask. Discipling, when done well, always gives the disciple the ability to overcome sin and temptation from the world, the flesh, and the devil. Furthermore, it turns the disciple into a person capable of discipling others.

How many churches disciple men and women and do it well? The answer is people who give money but rarely their time and gifts to build up others spiritually. When building up people is not everyone's responsibility, the church is not fulfilling its divine calling.

# Chapter 11

## THE CHURCH JESUS BUILDS
### Why the Church in the West is Failing

This closing chapter is to you, my dear reader, who has undertaken to read this book, hoping that you would find the truth within. Some topics have already been covered, but from a different perspective, and because changing views can give some the out, they need to dismiss the argument and say you're wrong. Nevertheless, if a statement is correct from differing angles, it can make the argument stronger. The Bible is the most influential book ever written because all angles are covered, and they all come to the same conclusion.

We all understand something new because of or despite what we believed before. If our previous belief was untrue, it placed us in a box of unbelief. Let us consider an example from the Apostle Paul, 2 Corinthians 4:6, "For God, who said, "Light shall shine out of darkness," is the One who has shone in our hearts to give the light of the knowledge of the glory of God in the face of Christ."

Paul begins his statement with God, who performs a miracle by causing light to shine out of the darkness. Typically, light dispels darkness, but in this verse, light shines out of the darkness. We are reminded of our Lord's words when He said in Matthew 6:23, "If the light that is in you is darkness, how great is that darkness." According to a Greek scholar, darkened (i.e., if the soul has lost its perceptive power), how great is the darkness." Light can be understood as truth, and darkness as its absence.

Let us return to the idea of living in a box. Each reader has a preconceived understanding of the Church. What you think you know could bind you in a lie rather than set you free in the truth. The old adage is correct. "It's not what you know that can hurt you, it's what you know that ain't so." We believe ourselves to see the truth, but if that were always true, God would never have to cause light to shine out of the darkness. Our entrance into the Kingdom of Light is a miracle. It always takes a miracle to think outside the box.

What is the box out of which the writer would like his readers to think? Beginning with the Church in the fourth Century, believers started down the wrong road. The road had two sides; we will only consider one side. The first side of the road consisted of understanding the scriptures mystically, spiritually, and not literally; that was a huge mistake. The men of the Reformation dispelled that box, and the Church set the Gospel free. The second side was a structure directly contradicting our Lord's teachings in Matthew 23 and the New Testament. There is a military element to the New Testament, but the ground is always level at the cross. I mean this: there is neither general nor pope, private nor pew sitter in Christianity. There can be learned and ignorant, laboring and slothful, but not by God's design. Jesus Christ died for all those He destined to eternal life, and all have an equal responsibility to live accordingly. There are gifts of the Holy Spirit that differ in degree according to God's grace bestowed (Romans 12), but these are not determined by church structure because when they are, they distort God's design.

I attended a church briefly where the preaching was reformed, biblical, and applicable. During one sermon, he said, "We do not dialogue with people; we proclaim the truth. This method he explained in the context of teaching in the Church. It was that way in a sermon or teaching in class. Questions were allowed at the end, but there were no conversational interactions. Here's the problem! In Acts 20:7, we read, "On the first day of the week, when we were gathered together to break bread, Paul *began* **talking** to them..." The word in *The Greek "dialégomai* means ("getting a conclusion across") and occurs 13 times in the NT, usually of believers exercising "dialectical reasoning." This is the process of *giving and receiving* information with someone to *reach a deeper understanding* – a "going back-and-forth" of thoughts and ideas so people can better know the Lord (His word, will). Doing this is perhaps the most telling characteristic of the growing Christian!"

It is not just this extreme case that distorts the New

Testament picture of the Church Jesus builds; it is much more. My proof from scripture will be the Church, as recorded on the pages of the New Testament.

# The House Church

If my readers live in many parts of the East, they are acquainted with house churches. Churches must stay small in certain parts of the world to avoid persecution. Some people feel more comfortable in a big church, while others like small churches. Let's consider why people fear or resist attending a house church. It's easy to slip in and slip out of a big church. "I don't want anyone putting their nose into my affairs." "I don't wish to inform anyone of how little I know about the Bible." "I don't want to be judged." "I don't want anyone to think I'm not a Christian." You get the idea.

We should answer two questions about house churches in the New Testament. The presence of the Holy Spirit was among the people for salvation; there was much love and grace. So much so that we read, in Acts 2:44, "those who had believed were together and had all things in common." The love shared during the early days after Pentecost was extraordinary and present among all the people. Acts 2:45, "...and they began selling their property and possessions and were sharing them **with all, as anyone might have need.**"

Furthermore, "...breaking bread from house to house, they

were taking their meals together with gladness and sincerity of heart…" How many people would want to avoid joining such a group? The answer is in verse 47, "praising God and having favor with all the people." All the people found the testimony of these early Christians favorable. Until, "And on that day a great persecution began against the Church in Jerusalem, and they were all scattered throughout the regions of Judea and Samaria, except the apostles. *Some* devout men buried Stephen, and made loud lamentations over him. But Saul *began* ravaging the Church, entering house after house, and dragging off men and women, he would put them in prison" Acts 8:1-3.

The accounts from the Book of Acts reveal that it was in the Temple that evangelism took place. We are not told where they were on the Day of Pentecost, except it had to accommodate thousands of people. In Acts 1, one hundred people met in the upper room where they were staying.

At the Church's founding, people could live in a small place like a house on the prairie or a compound that accommodates many people. There were no church buildings. In Colossians 4:15, "Greet the brethren who are in Laodicea and also Nympha and the church that is in her house."

In Acts 16:14-15, a woman named Lydia received Christ, "A woman named Lydia, from the city of Thyatira, a seller of purple fabrics, a worshiper of God, was listening; and the Lord opened her heart to respond to the things spoken by Paul. And when she and her household had been baptized, she urged us, saying, "If you have judged me to be faithful to the Lord, come into my house and stay." And she prevailed upon us." We are not told the size of her household, but it could accommodate Paul's party. It became a place for them to stay, which they did after leaving the prison; in verse 40, "They went out of the prison and entered *the house of* Lydia, and when they saw the brethren, they encouraged them and departed."

Undoubtedly, Caesar's house could have held many people, but we do not know how many believers resided there. "The brethren who are with me greet you. All the saints greet you, especially those of Caesar's household." Philippians 4:21, 22.

The New Testament only refers to the Church as people, as in Romans 16:3-5, "Greet Prisca and Aquila, my fellow workers in Christ Jesus, who for my life risked their own necks, to whom not only do I give thanks, but also all the churches of the Gentiles; also greet the church that is in their house." Please notice that **the Church was in their house. The Church was not the building; the Church was in the building.**

**Reputation often preceded people as they gave themselves to serve the Church.** Romans 16:1-2 "I commend to you our sister Phoebe, who is a servant of the church which is at Cenchrea; that you receive her in the Lord in a manner worthy of the saints, and that you help her in whatever manner she may have need of you; for she herself has also been a helper of many, and of myself as well."

Furthermore, some servants were willing to risk their lives

to help fellow servants of Christ. Romans 16:3-16 "Greet Prisca and Aquila, my fellow workers in Christ Jesus, 4who for my life risked their own necks, to whom not only do I give thanks, but also all the churches of the Gentiles; also greet the church that is in their house." Of course, the Church was in their house." **A beneficial feature of a house church is the owner covers the cost. The person who lives in it covers money that would go to an additional building for worship service once a week. More money can go to feed people experiencing poverty and ministry work.**

From Romans 16, we have a lineup of special people to Paul and, therefore, to all those in the household of faith. He tells the Church in Rome to greet these people, which in Greek is to welcome or feel comfortable, draw to oneself, unite with, wish well, or love as you love yourself. He names the first convert first. These are transformed people and part of a new family. Mary worked hard, and Andronicus and Junias were fellow prisoners with Paul or giving themselves to Christ through persecution. Ampliatus was said to be beloved of the Lord. Some will say, are not all people loved by the Lord? We should never contend with the word of God; God singled out a person who is said to be beloved. We may need to rethink the beloved of the Lord. Urbanus was a fellow worker, Stachys, beloved by Paul. Apelles were approved in Christ, *dókimos in Greek or* "to receive what passes the necessary test scrutinized; hence *acceptable* because *genuine.*

Then Paul points out other households of Aristobulus and

also Narcissus. There were Tryphaena and Tryphosa, referred to as workers. Christianity is about working for God; it is not receiving from Him and then going about our lives as if nothing changed. Rufus was referred to as a choice man. A judgment is coming, and on that day, we will prefer to be referred to with an attribute attached to us so we won't be regarded as worthless in work, not for others to hear but as coming from Jesus Christ. The last names have no attributes.

In Romans Romans 16:23, we learn of "Gaius, host to me and to the whole church, greets you." The whole Church benefited from the generosity and courage of Gaius, who hosted a persecuted church.

The New Testament writers inspired by God set the pattern of house churches. The change did not come until the dim beginnings of the Middle Ages when kings and popes used Christianity and God as a means of ordained authority for their rule.

Some will ask, how is the Church to maintain sound doctrine? Let me remind all the nay-sayers against house churches that the Church is anything but united about doctrine. Each denomination has its own seminaries and specific teachings that differ from others. If it is a unity you desire, which you should, don't look to sects that divide.

From where does unity come? I do not intend to be super spiritual at this point or over-simplify a crucial matter in church life. However, dependence upon God over and above that of leaders cannot be over-emphasized. Pride in leadership is ubiquitous, and pride is destructive. Of course, leadership is essential to the Church, but its arrogance must be curtailed. Furthermore, the 80/20 rule must be eliminated from church life because it is not according to God's design. God died for every born-again believer, exhausting the same suffering for all; therefore, all are accountable to go and make disciples.

## A House Church Must Have Spirit-filled Believers

Let's consider unity and leadership from God's design in Ephesians 4:4-6, "*There is* one body and one Spirit, just as also you were called in one hope of your calling; one Lord, one faith, one baptism, one God and Father of all who is over all and through all and in all." So then, why is the Church fractured into a thousand pieces? First, not all the Church is of God any more than all Israel is descended from Israel. (Romans 9:6) Because a person is born in a bakery does not make them a bagel. Rebirth is required for membership in God's family. (John 3:3) Second, the fullness of Christ is necessary for all to be in complete unity. The filling of the Spirit is a topic that needs to be understood and applied.

The Apostle Paul told the Ephesians church the same thing in 5:13-18. "But all things become visible when they are exposed by the light, for everything that becomes visible is light. For this reason it says, "Awake, sleeper, and arise from the dead, and Christ will shine on you." So then, be careful how you walk, not as unwise people but as wise, making the most of your time, because the days are evil. Therefore do not be foolish, but understand what the will of the Lord *is*. And do not get drunk with wine, in which there is debauchery, but be filled with the Spirit..."

The Church does not need more seminaries that are technically accurate, perhaps, but rarely enlightened and empowered by the Spirit of God. How do I know this? Where the Spirit of God is present, there is unity. In context, Ephesians 4:4 begins by saying, "There is one body and one Spirit," with capital "S." Where there is One Spirit of God, who is God, in the person of the Holy Spirit, there is one Church, when all the people are filled with Him. Seminaries do not accomplish this; God does! How? **I refer my readers to The Calvary Road by Roy Hession for this answer.**

Roy Hession was a missionary in East Africa during a revival in the mid-twentieth Century. Revival is always exhilarating and, at the same time, extremely humbling. People only come to the cross for salvation as destitute of morality and helpless sinners. Nothing is humbling like understanding that you are worthless, helpless, hopeless, and far more wretched in the eyes of the infinitely holy, righteous, and eternal God than you could ever imagine. Nevertheless, the only way to be filled with the Holy Spirit is to be moved to the cross through the awareness of your sins.

The Bible speaks to believers about a filling of the Spirit on an ongoing basis. Rebirth is a one-time occurrence; it regenerates the soul and spirit of a person so that God can live within them and move anew once again. The first time was at the creation of Adam in the Garden, Genesis 2:7, "Then the LORD God formed man of dust from the ground, and breathed into his nostrils the breath of life; and man became a living being." When Adam and Eve sinned, spiritual life was lost even though they continued biologically. Paul teaches us about this state of spiritual death in Colossians 2:13, "When you were dead in your transgressions and the uncircumcision of your flesh, He made you alive together with Him, having forgiven us all our transgressions."

Circumcision was an ordinance signifying a separation from the world and to God, which happens spiritually when a person is born again by God's grace. Before rebirth, we were dead in transgressions, not biologically but spiritually. We are made alive once and united to God at that moment. Sin can still separate us from God's presence, and His spiritual guidance and internal voice grow faint.

**Ephesians 5:17 teaches us,** "Do not get drunk with wine, for that is dissipation, but be filled with the Spirit." "Be filled" is in the present continuous tense and could read "be, being filled." God never takes His Spirit from the redeemed, but He does distance Himself when believers persist in willful and unrepentant sin. Believers are wrongly taught about the ministry of the Holy Spirit, whether Baptist or Charismatic and everyone else. To one extent or another, it is rarely articulated today that sin is a wedge-driving force between the presence of God and a believer experiencing Holy Spirit power.

Believe it or not, the effect on Old Testament saints dealing with the Philistines or New Testament saints proclaiming the Gospel is the same. The experience of Samson, Judges 16:20, a hero of faith found in Hebrews chapter eleven, like virtually all Old Testament saints, gives us a perfect example. "She said, "The Philistines are upon you, Samson!" And he awoke from his sleep and said, "I will go out as at other times and shake myself free." But he did not know that the LORD had departed from him." The sin doesn't have to be sleeping with a prostitute or even immorality; it could just be pride that causes the absence of God's presence with power.

The Old Testament is primarily the story of God's chosen people, Israel. Within the nation, as Paul elaborates in Romans 9 to 11, all descendants of Abraham are Israel. However, only a remnant with the faith of Abraham is the predetermined, saved, elected children according to the promise of redemption in Jesus Christ. Those children are the Abrahams, Moses, Samuels, Davids, and the prophets. All others carry the name only but are as lost as Gentiles before the Church. Within Christianity, many assume the standing but are as rejected as the nation of Israel. However, those who experience rebirth, which comes first, also possess saving faith.

A person with saving faith, as Samson, can judge Israel for twenty years as he did but stray from the faith and, as we have seen, have God depart from him for a time. The Holy Spirit does not part with the loss of salvation; God will never break His promise to save, but the power is lost. Therefore, when God speaks to Israel in Isaiah 59:1-3, for example, He speaks to the nation, not the remnant. "Behold, the LORD'S hand is not so short that it cannot save; nor is His ear so dull that it cannot hear. But your iniquities have made a separation between you and your God, and your sins have hidden *His* face from you so that He does not hear. For your hands are defiled with blood and your fingers with iniquity."

God is speaking to the saved in name only, and their lives prove their lack of transformation. The chapter does not end there but continues in verses fifteen to seventeen, "Now the LORD saw, and it was displeasing in His sight that there was no justice. And He saw that there was no man, and was astonished that there was no one to intercede; then His own arm brought salvation to Him, and His righteousness upheld Him. He put on righteousness like a breastplate, and a helmet of salvation on His head." How this change takes place is described in verses twenty and twenty-one. "A Redeemer will come to Zion, and to those who turn from transgression in Jacob," declares the LORD. "As for Me, this is My covenant with them," says the LORD: "My Spirit which is upon you, and My words which I have put in your mouth shall not depart from your mouth."

God frequently speaks of salvation and the accompaniment of the Holy Spirit. There is a transformation in every person upon rebirth and saving faith. Yet, there must be a walk in the Spirit, dependence upon Him, a fullness of discipleship in an understanding of the authentic Gospel, the fellowship of the saints, and a continual humbling of oneself to stand against the warring forces of the world, the flesh, and the devil.

Discipleship is mainly about giving brothers and sisters in Christ the weapons to fight the battles against the world, the flesh, and the devil. It encourages the weary, cares for the wounded, edifies the brokenhearted, and loves the mistreated. When discipleship is done for God's glory, it must be done as Jesus did. Jesus chose twelve men that the Father gave to Him. It was an act of cooperation. Jesus did not teach facts unconnected to real-life experience. Jesus lived out His life choices, his words, the manner he spoke, the laws He obeyed, and the scripture He honored before His disciples. Further, He did so in proximity that made observing Him possible. Such discipleship between a congregation, a single pastor, and a few elders is impossible.

## A House Church Must Produce Believers Who Disciple Others

The only accurate way to understand New Testament ministry is through the lens of discipleship. Upon His departure, in the presence of the eleven Apostles, Jesus gave the Church the meaning and means of ministry. "All authority has been given to Me in heaven and on earth. "Go therefore and make disciples of all the nations, baptizing them in the name of the Father and the Son and the Holy Spirit, teaching them to observe all that I commanded you; and lo, I am with you always, even to the end of the age," Matthew 28:18, 19.

On a Sunday after Church, a young man asked if we could spend lunch together, so I invited him over to the house; that was a common occurrence in those days. We were sitting on the couch, and he asked me, "Would you disciple me?" I wondered why he chose me, and he replied, "Because I heard you pray." Four or five years later, he called from the seminary and said to me, "I asked a professor if he would disciple me, and he said, 'I wouldn't know where to start.'" Therein lies the problem: even seminary professors need to learn how to disciple.

Before I explain discipleship and how it's done, we must make an exception to the rule of house church leadership. The following is the exception and not the rule.

**The Exception to House Churches**, and there are very few, let me say that again, very few. God gave twelve men to the first generation of church life. We know there are only twelve because there are only twelve foundation stones for the New Jerusalem with their names on them. End of story! There are no small "a" apostles; God gave Apostles, and there were twelve. God gave Aurelius Augustinus Hipponensis, known as Saint Augustin, born November 13, 354, in Tagaste, Numidia [now

Souk Ahras, Algeria]—died August 28, 430. God sent him to help direct the Church; he was not perfect or even an Apostle. The devil repeatedly uses the best men to make gross errors, which the Apostles did not do. There are the Luthers, Calvins, Spurgeons, and Martin Lloyd Joneses, but they are few and far between. There are men with huge congregations that mean nothing when the Church is intended to meet in a house. That is it for exceptions.

**Why a House Church Must Be A Family.** A church is meant to behave like a family. In Mark chapter 3, Jesus chose twelve men to be with him and who would follow Him. Then He returned home, and when His family arrived, they called for Him because a crowd had formed. When the crowd informed Jesus of His family, we are told, "Looking about at those who were sitting around Him, He said, "Behold My mother and My brothers! "For whoever does the will of God, he is My brother and sister and mother." Jesus' disciples, by His testimony, were His family, and he treated them as such.

The results of Christian family gatherings are mainly missing in American church culture. That is not to say there is never good fellowship, fun, and sometimes personal interactions, depending upon the Church. Nevertheless, when a church functions from week to week or day to day as a family, loving, caring, nurturing, building one another up, and holding one another accountable, as things are done in a healthy, well-adjusted family, the benefits far outweigh a building that gathers people who hardly speak to one another except for what can be counted in minutes on a Sunday morning or a special occasion.

Discipleship is about believers interacting around the word of God to understand how God interacts with His people through joyful and sorrowful times. It helps doctrine become the soul by which healthy Christians interact in a world that opposes their thinking and lifestyle. A healthy family does not stop meeting together and loving each other because of differences. In Christ, there are no differences, and because there are so many differences in the Church, it begs the question of how well we are in Christ.

Denominations are anti-family. Some will say there are many differences in families. That is true because everyone has the right to believe what they want. In the Church or Christ's family, Christians only have the right to be what Christ wants. When the final judgment is over, the saints are perfected in holiness, and the New Jerusalem has descended from the new heaven to the new earth. Revelation 22:3 says, "There will no longer be any curse, and the throne of God and the Lamb will be in it, and His slaves will serve Him."

The family of God are slaves of love and righteousness to Christ. Why not start here and now and stop making excuses because we're imperfect? Why not become students of Christ by replacing false teachings and teachers? Because the Gospel God gave back to the Church during the Reformation is so different from what is preached today, why not understand what happened then and return to it? Do "Christians" no longer believe that Satan is in the business of detracting from the Church the truth to make it impotent? People need to think outside the box, properly love and respect Jesus Christ, and come together as the family they are.

## A House Church Must Be Committed to the Lordship of Jesus Christ

We considered the word discipline that Paul used to describe the order in the Church that exalts Christ properly. The very next verse stated by Paul to the Colossian Church in 2:6 says, "Therefore as you have received Christ Jesus the Lord, so walk in Him." The context previously and following this statement overwhelmingly speaks of exalting Jesus Christ in our minds and hearts as our first, last, and only priority. When Paul says, 'as you have received Christ Jesus the Lord he by the Spirit of God is bringing us back to the Day of Pentecost and Peter's sermon, "...let all the house of Israel know for certain that God has made Him both Lord and Christ—this Jesus whom you crucified" (2:36).

Some people love to call Jesus Christ by His first name, which is a good name as it means God is the savior, and it was that savior who, when dying, said, "Father, forgive them, for they know not what they are doing." That is, they are trying to destroy the means of their salvation. So many today call God

Jesus, not knowing who He is. He is the human being God made Lord, that is, Master in a slave-master relationship, and Christ, that is, the anointed, messiah or sent one, being the second person of the triune God. Paul, therefore, says to us, "As you have received Christ (the sent) Jesus (Savior) the Lord (and Master), even so, walk in Him."

John Newton penned, "Twas grace that taught my heart to fear." Did we receive Christ in fear? Just as importantly, do we walk in Him in fear? In the context that everyone shall bow to Christ as Lord, Paul tells us in Philippians 2:12, 13, "Work out your salvation with fear and trembling; for it is God who is at work in you, both to will and to work for [His] good pleasure."

How do you know if you fear God and take His words seriously? If you live in a "church" box and are resolved in your belief, though it is found untrue, which is an unteachable spirit, then the following verses and reasoning will not change your mind.

Paul continues exalting Christ and making Him central to every part of life for the Christian in Colossians two and halfway down chapter three. He then introduces us to body life from verses twelve to seventeen, "So, as those who have been chosen of God...

**Chosen does not mean God chose us because we first chose Him; Jesus said, "You did not choose Me, but I chose you, and appointed you that you would go and bear fruit and that your fruit would remain..." (John 15:16). We are not**

sovereign over anything in God's universe, He is sovereign over everything, including our salvation.

Therefore, Paul continues, "...holy and beloved, put on a heart of compassion, kindness, humility, gentleness and patience; bearing with one another, and forgiving each other, whoever has a complaint against anyone; just as the Lord forgave you, so should you."

**Such body life as just sighted is not about internal disputes over the rug's color among a people of luxury; it refers to a vibrant church accosted by satanically motivated spiritual warfare while persecuted by the world on the outside.**

Paul continues, "...and Beyond all these things, put on love, which is the perfect bond of unity..."

**Those seeking unity are people unwilling to accept defeat on the battlefield of denominational snobbery and pride. They are discontent to call what they have in their group of a hundred or 10,000 unity when they remain at odds with countless believers worldwide. Unity seekers never stop praying for the unity that Jesus Christ desires.**

Paul would never suggest compromise on such a subject as unity. He continues, "Let the peace of Christ rule in your hearts, to which indeed you were called in one body, and be thankful. Let the word of Christ richly dwell within you, with all wisdom teaching and admonishing one another with psalms and hymns and spiritual songs, singing with thankfulness in your hearts to God. Whatever you do in word or deed, do all in the name of the Lord Jesus, giving thanks through Him to God the Father."

My dear readers understand that "...with all wisdom teaching and admonishing one another with psalms and hymns and spiritual songs, singing with thankfulness in your hearts to God." is not speaking to an hour service on a Sunday morning alone. Why? Because it is attached to, "Whatever you do in word or deed, do all in the name of the Lord Jesus, giving thanks through Him to God the Father." Discipleship never ends like fellowship never ends; it is not an hour-long sermon, a college class, or a seminary degree. Biblical fellowship built upon self-sacrificing discipleship binds the ties so tightly they can never be broken.

## Church Leaders Must Be Humble

Pride ruins everything! Paul referred to two kinds of people preaching the Gospel in his letter to the Philippians when he wrote, in 1:15-18, "Some, to be sure, are preaching Christ even from envy and strife, but some also from good will; the latter do it out of love, knowing that I am appointed for the defense of the Gospel; the former proclaim Christ out of selfish ambition rather than from pure motives, thinking to cause me distress in my imprisonment. What then? Only that in every way, whether in pretense or in truth, Christ is proclaimed; and in this I rejoice."

Paul rejoiced because of the proclamation of the Gospel regardless of motive. He understood strife in his distress in the Church even at that early date. One group was moving in God's perfect will, while others in Phippi fell to pride in themselves and became casualties to the devil's lies. It is essential to understand that those attacking Paul in his suffering were brothers in Christ. Paul would never have rejoiced in the preaching of a false Gospel. He could not have spoken about false teachers any worse than he did in Galatians 1, "I am amazed that you are so quickly deserting Him who called you by the grace of Christ, for a different gospel; which is *really* not another; only there are some who are disturbing you and want to distort the Gospel of Christ. But even if we, or an angel from heaven, should preach to you a gospel contrary to what we have preached to you, he is to be accursed!"

He brought one of the worst curses on the false teachers in the Galatian churches by saying they should be incapable of being redeemed. Then, to ensure his readers don't mistake what he said, he repeats the curse in verse nine. He would never have pronounced such a curse on a person he believed to be a brother in Christ.

Then, in his letters to the Ephesians and Colossians, he placed Christ in His rightful place as head of the Church (Col. 1:18 and Eph. 5:23). By head, Paul meant above all, through all, in all, and all in all in (Eph. 4:5 and Col. 3:11). Why is this point made and expanded upon by Paul? Unless the Church understands Jesus Christ in His rightful place, men lose sight of to whom and what they are in relation.

At the heart of Colossians 1 and central in the text (verses

15-20 is a focused summation of Christ's exaltation over all His creation and supremacy in what He redeems. "He is the image of the invisible God, the firstborn of all creation. For by Him all things were created, both in the heavens and on earth, visible and invisible, whether thrones or dominions or rulers or authorities—all things have been created through Him and for Him. He is before all things, and in Him all things hold together. He is also head of the body, the Church; and He is the beginning, the firstborn from the dead, so that He Himself will come to have first place in everything. For it was the Father's good pleasure for all the fullness to dwell in Him, and through Him to reconcile all things to Himself, having made peace through the blood of His cross; through Him, I say, whether things on earth or things in heaven."

Paul's chief concern throughout the Colossian letter is to make Christ central and supreme in everything so that through Him, believers might attain a fullness experienced no other way, Col. 2:1-5, "For I want you to know how great a struggle I have on your behalf and for those who are at Laodicea, and for all those who have not personally seen my face, that their hearts may be encouraged, having been knit together in love, and attaining to all the wealth that comes from the full assurance of understanding, resulting in a true knowledge of God's mystery, that is, Christ Himself, in whom are hidden all the treasures of wisdom and knowledge. I say this so that no one will delude you with persuasive arguments. For even though I am absent in body, nevertheless, I am with you in Spirit, rejoicing to see your good discipline and the stability of your faith in Christ." **Faith in Christ depends on seeing Christ as He is and not how the devil would distort Him in our thinking.**

Please note verse 5, "...your good discipline and the stability of your faith." Discipline or Táksis in Greek is derived from tássō, which is to arrange or order. It is to place one member over another in rank. A Greek scholar said it this way, "taksis, as an ancient military term, describes an ordered troop ("cohort") – arranged in descending rank. This term suggests a detailed ordering rather than simply a general disposition of an army."

By this definition, we would understand the Church as an army and not as Jesus described it in Matthew 23, where he tells the disciples not to be called doctors or professors by anyone and to call no one their father. These directions Jesus gave to the Church so that God would remain in supremacy by the Church and the ground would remain level at the cross. A hierarchy does not allow Christ's sacrifice to be administered equally to, over, and in all. The scripture cannot refer to gifts at this juncture but the efficacy of the blood of Christ; neither can the word of God contradict Himself.

So then, what is meant by discipline? That was my question upon viewing this term in my quiet time. The answer came as I continued to investigate. **"order, i. e. a fixed succession also observing a fixed time." and reference given was Luke 1:8.** The context of this verse is referencing Zacharias, the father of

John the Baptist. Therefore, in Luke 1:8 and 9, we read, "Now it happened that while he was performing his priestly service before God in the appointed order of his division, according to the custom of the priestly office, he was chosen by lot the priests to enter the temple of the Lord and burn incense." God so ordered by the priesthood and lot Zacharias for this specific time. Only priests from the line of Aaron were allowed to serve in the Temple and narrowed to one by picking a lot or short straw in our vernacular.

The only priest referred to in the New Testament as Our Great High Priest is Our Lord Jesus Christ. The only reference to discipline outside of priesthood is 1 Corinthians 14:40, referring to how things should be done in an orderly manner and without confusion. When people are filled with the Holy Spirit, who is not confused, they behave orderly. The Church is orderly when Jesus is at the head where He belongs.

All the remaining verses using taksis are in the letter to the Hebrews concerning Jesus Christ as our High Priest and referencing His being a priest in the order of Melchizedek, which is not of the line of human priests as was Zacharias. Even a superficial reading of the New Testament will eliminate the presence of priests as ministers, bishops, cardinals, or popes. The Bible uses the name priest but focuses on the function. Are there leaders? As sure as there are men who study scripture. The separation of believers to leadership is those who rightly divide God's word from those who can't because of youth, lack of study, corruption of understanding for various reasons, or not being a regenerate believer. What must be remembered is that the qualified leader lives what they teach.

When the exalted Christ is head of the Church, its appearance becomes like the day of Pentecost minus the Apostles.

# Chapter 12

## THE CHURCH JESUS BUILDS PART 2
### Why the Church in the West is Failing

Many things can come to mind when the word worship is mentioned. In many church circles today, worship conjures up the idea of music. However, worship is any word, action, feeling, attitude, or motive directed to please the creator God and to give Him praise, honor, and glory in a spirit of thanksgiving.

Worship can be done alone in a closet, but church worship is intended to be participatory. The Church is the body of Christ, and as such, it has many members; 1 Corinthians 12:12 says, "For even as the body is one and yet has many members, and all the members of the body, though they are many, are one body, so also is Christ." The Church functions inside and outside of the day of worship. It is easy to confuse church life as if it were only within a building on a Sunday. Also, the spiritual gifts given to people are not only to function on the day of worship but even more so the rest of the week. Discipleship, for instance, may or may not take place on a Sunday, and all are called to disciple. We know this from Matthew 28:18-20.

"All authority has been given to Me in heaven and on earth. "Go therefore and make disciples of all the nations, baptizing them in the name of the Father and the Son and the Holy Spirit, teaching them to observe all that I commanded you; and lo, I am with you always, even to the end of the age."

Any well-adjusted person blessed with the gift of a child knows the joys and responsibilities attached to the privilege. What a colossal rip-off that discipleship should be assigned by church people and leaders to those with seminary training and a desire to lead in that particular way. My dear readers, please understand that I am not skirting the need to learn the scriptures well. I am expressing that as multitudes of people start families and work hard at nurturing, teaching, and exemplifying maturity. The next generation grows up and does the same thing. In America, teachers have been high-jacking parents' primary responsibility to train a child in the way they should go. In the same way, whether they realize it or not, church leaders do the same thing.

When the local body of Christ comes together on the day of worship, the gathering time will only be as good as the people who come together to worship. If the members are filled with the Holy Spirit, if they have been prayerful, if they are transparent, if they are prepared to share from God's word, to prophesy, praise, pray, teach, prophecy, and share a word of knowledge, then it will be an exciting and fruitful time. If not, it could face the same report Corinth received from Paul.

Sunday worship time is no more for professionals than eleven ordinary and sinful men chosen to be Apostles. Again, my dear readers, I agree that God raises men in every generation to speak more clearly than the rest on matters of the Church and the Kingdom of God. There are the Luthers, Calvins, Spurgeons, Martin Lloyd Jones, etc., for particular direction changes. The Church always goes off track in many ways; if it didn't, such men would not be needed. However, instead of fighting the battles with leaders only, as the Church does, the war is meant to be won by an army.

Think of a church where, on a Sunday morning, the people were eager to give testimony, share a word from God, teach a scripture that made their week better, and in many other ways, all for the edification of others and not for any selfish reason. Paul taught well what is essential when the body comes together for worship. 1 Corinthians 14:6, "But now, brethren, if I come to you speaking in tongues, what will I profit you unless I speak to you either by way of **revelation** or of **knowledge** or of **prophecy** or of teaching?"

The Church is not to be just a classroom. Teaching is good, but there should be so much more. Revelation is the manifestation of Jesus Christ, which He reveals through the members of His body. When God is allowed to work in people, when they are not trying to usurp the Holy Spirit's ministry, extraordinary things occur. Knowledge (gnósis) is functional working knowledge gleaned from first-hand experience by connecting theory to application through a direct relationship. Prophecy - prophétēs, makes clear and asserts as a priority what is clarified by divinely-empowered forth-telling from scripture and proclaiming the mind of God.

Teaching - didáskō establishes education that summarizes known teaching that does not compromise God's word.

Quench not the Spirit is quickly accomplished when God cannot draw near. The illustration I love the most is that on the day of Jesus' baptism, the Holy Spirit was seen by John the Baptist descending as a dove, which landed upon the Lamb of God. The lamb is willing to be Shorn; it does not fight back or defend itself. Only when such an attitude is in the people of God does the Holy Spirit make His presence known.

Some years ago, I and a group of men would meet from time to time from 3 a.m. until eight or nine o'clock. On the first occasion, I quoted from Mark 1:35, "In the early morning, while it was still dark, Jesus got up, left the house, and went away to a secluded place, and was praying there." I divided an allotment of times and length so we wouldn't walk on one another's prayer time. I divided the time into worship, praise, thanksgiving, confession, and intercession. These were not set as rules but as guidelines. Everyone prayed in the spirit because they were all there to meet with God. It always turned out to be an exceptional time, as it always does, when God draws near.

The men were always picked because I knew they were honest and not hypocritical. I once chose to give a man a chance, but deep down, I had doubts, and he brought the entire spirit to a bad place. I often asked others to attend, wondering if they would help or hurt the spirit of prayer, and nearly always, they did not show. Once, I stopped to ask a pastor if he would attend, and he told me he would fall asleep if he did.

Sunday morning worship is about meeting with God; it's not about feelings, but they should be part of the meeting experience. Jeremiah tells us in 29:13," "You will seek Me and find *Me* when you search for Me with all your heart." Many scriptures confirm that man was made with intellect, emotions, and will. Many verses from the Old and the New Testaments confirm the Jewish mindset of the heart. The writer of the Hebrews refers to the total man in this way: 10:16, "This is the covenant that I will make with them after those days, say the LORD: I will put my laws upon their heat, and on their mind I will write them."

The mind is included in the heart and thereby mentioned twice in the covenant of promise. A Person's choices are best made through the intellect and not emotions because God always reasons first. When the reason is sound, the feelings of the spirit-filled man will follow.

Worship cannot be man-centered but must point those gathered to God, the creator and redeemer. When the house is filled with spirit-filled worshippers, it can only be exciting and heart-warming, so joy is the overwhelming experience. There may be tears from sad stories, but the brethren will be there for others, not themselves.

## A Closing Word of Warning

The 20th Century brought abuses of many kinds concerning the expression of the Church. Learning, as well as emotionalism, have been significantly abused. People always look for signs of God's presence when it never becomes clearer than when sin is acknowledged and brought to the cross for confession and cleansing. A verse I only hear seldom is Matthew 16:4, "An evil and adulterous generation seeks after a sign; and a sign will not be given it, except the sign of Jonah." And He left them and went away."

God should never be put to the test as to his existence. He exists in every man's conscience unless he has become so insensitive that he can no longer hear it. We are told many times and in many ways that the Christian is to walk by faith and not by sight. Therefore, when we wait on God in prayer, the most significant expression of our faith, and we do so in a sincere and honest spirit of belief, He will hear and make His presence known.

# A House Church Must
# Endorse Biblical Discipline

After the historical record of the four Gospels and The Acts of the Apostles, Paul launches into the most focused and extensive explanation of Christian teaching and its application in his letter to the Romans. He then deals with a sinful license in two letters to the Corinthian Church and legalism to the churches of Galatia. The letters to the Ephesians and the Colossians bookend his letter to the Philippians. Paul referred to two kinds of people preaching the Gospel to those at Philippi when he wrote, in 1:15-18, "Some, to be sure, are preaching Christ even from envy and strife, but some also from good will; the latter *do it* out of love, knowing that I am appointed for the defense of the Gospel; the former proclaim Christ out of selfish ambition rather than from pure motives, thinking to cause me distress in my imprisonment. What then? Only that in every way, whether in pretense or in truth, Christ is proclaimed; and in this I rejoice."

Paul rejoiced because of the proclamation of the Gospel regardless of motive. He understood strife in his distress in the Church even at that early date. One group was moving in God's perfect will, and like those at Corinth and Galatia, the devil had his triumphs.

Then, in his letters to the Ephesians and Colossians, he placed Christ in his rightful place as head of the Church (Col.

1:18 and Eph. 5:23). By head, Paul meant above all, through all, and in all and also all in all (Eph. 4:5 and Col. 3:11). Why is this point made and expanded upon by Paul? Unless the Church understands Jesus Christ in His rightful place, men lose sight of who and what they are in relation to Him.

At the heart of Colossians 1 and central in the text (verses 15-20 is a focused summation of Christ's exaltation over all His creation and supremacy in what He redeems. "He is the image of the invisible God, the firstborn of all creation. For by Him all things were created, *both* in the heavens and on earth, visible and invisible, whether thrones or dominions or rulers or authorities—all things have been created through Him and for Him. He is before all things, and in Him all things hold together. He is also head of the body, the Church; and He is the beginning, the firstborn from the dead, so that He Himself will come to have first place in everything. For it was the *Father's* good pleasure for all the fullness to dwell in Him, and through Him to reconcile all things to Himself, having made peace through the blood of His cross; through Him, *I say,* whether things on earth or things in heaven."

Paul's chief concern throughout the Colossian letter is to make Christ central and supreme in everything so that through Him, believers might attain a fullness experienced no other way, Col. 2:1-5, "For I want you to know how great a struggle I have on your behalf and for those who are at Laodicea, and for all those who have not personally seen my face, that their hearts may be encouraged, having been knit together in love, and *attaining* to all the wealth that comes from the full assurance of understanding, *resulting* in a true knowledge of God's mystery, *that is,* Christ *Himself,* in whom are hidden all the treasures of wisdom and knowledge. I say this so that no one will delude you with persuasive arguments. For even though I am absent in body, nevertheless, I am with you in spirit, rejoicing to see your good discipline and the stability of your faith in Christ." Faith in Christ depends on seeing Christ as He is and not how the devil would distort Him in our thinking.

Please note verse 5, "…your good discipline and the stability of your faith." Discipline or *Táksis* in Greek is derived from *tássō, which is* to arrange or order. It is to place one member *over* another in rank. A Greek scholar said it this way, "*taksis,* as an ancient military term, describes an *ordered troop* ("cohort") – *arranged in* descending *rank.* This term suggests a *detailed* ordering rather than simply a general *disposition* of an army."

By this definition, we would understand the Church as an army and not as Jesus described it in Matthew 23, where he tells the disciples not to be called doctors or professors by anyone and to call no one their father. These directions Jesus gave to the Church so that God would remain in supremacy by the Church and the ground would remain level at the cross. A hierarchy does not allow Christ's sacrifice to be administered equally to, over, and in all. The scripture cannot refer to gifts at this juncture but the efficacy of the blood of Christ; neither can the word of God contradict Himself.

So then, what is meant by discipline? That was my question upon viewing this term in my quiet time. The answer came as I continued to investigate. "order, i. e. a fixed succession also observing a fixed time." The reference given was Luke 1:8. The context of this verse is referencing Zacharias, the father of John the Baptist. Therefore, in Luke 1:8 and 9, we read, "Now it happened *that* while he was performing his priestly service before God in the *appointed* order of his division, according to the custom of the priestly office, he was chosen by lot the priests to enter the temple of the Lord and burn incense." God so ordered by the priesthood and lot Zacharias for this specific time. Only priests from the line of Aaron were allowed to serve in the Temple, and the only priest referred to in the New Testament as Our Great High Priest is our Lord Jesus Christ.

The only reference to discipline outside of priesthood is Corinthians 14:40, referring to how things should be done in an orderly manner and without confusion. When people are filled with the Holy Spirit, who is not confused, they behave orderly. The Church is orderly when Jesus is at the head where He belongs.

All the remaining verses are in the letter to the Hebrews concerning Jesus Christ as our High Priest and referencing His being a priest in the order of Melchizedek, which is not of the line of human priests as was Zacharias. Even a superficial reading of the New Testament will eliminate the presence of priests as ministers, bishops, cardinals, or popes. We are not speaking to the name of a minister but the function. Are there leaders? As sure as there are men who study scripture. The separation in the Bible concerning believers is those who can rightly divide God's word and those who can't because of youth, lack of study, corruption of understanding for various reasons, or not being a regenerate believer.

When the exalted Christ is head of the Church, its appearance becomes like the day of Pentecost minus the Apostles.

## The House Church Must Produce Leaders

If it is the passion of a church to disciple people to maturity in the faith, two things are vitally necessary. The first is that the Church gets the Gospel correct, and the second is an accurate understanding of maturity.

Many think they understand the Gospel because they know the basics, and being taught to keep it simple, they're good. Nevertheless, Paul, by the grace of God, was wise concerning character, and still, he was amazed, and said so in Galatians 1:6, "I am amazed that you are so quickly deserting Him who called you by the grace of Christ, for a different gospel."

He wasn't surprised they got it wrong; he was amazed at how quickly. It may be okay to keep the Gospel simple if that is what a person needs to hear, but many need much more. We need to be led by God in such things. Putting people into a one-size-fits-all may be suitable for clothes but not sharing the Gospel. Furthermore, Martin Luther said, concerning Paul's statement in 1 Corinthians 2:2, "I determined to know nothing among you except Jesus Christ, and Him crucified," he did not mean he would only stand on a corner and only proclaim Jesus Christ was crucified, but he would only proclaim the doctrines of Christ.

If you get the doctrines wrong, you get the Gospel wrong. If you get the Gospel wrong, you may end up with someone who looks and sounds like a Christian and is not. For this reason, Paul was exceedingly irritated with the Galatian error. The doctrine of Christ must be more than 1 Corinthians 15:3-4, "Christ died for our sins according to the Scriptures, and that He was buried, and that He was raised on the third day according to the Scriptures." It must be more than you are a sinner, trust Jesus, and you're in.

If you read the Life of George Whitefield by Dallimore, you will discover that, being taught theology at Oxford, he became so concerned about what was involved in salvation that he couldn't eat for a month and almost died. Whitefield was probably the most unction-filled preacher since the Apostle Paul. Some people need the whole truth, especially those who hear from hypocrites and twist the context with other false teachings.

What a person believes to enter the kingdom of God is also vital to their spiritual growth. There are doctrines and not just legalism that twist the grace of God into works, teachings about futile fleshly efforts to please God. These teachings differ slightly from the self-help books that the world produces; nevertheless, they can do equal damage to the believer's faith. It is always necessary that a person understand that all things, especially the means of grace, are from, through, and unto God's glory. Believers must understand the concept of grace correctly to ensure the stability of their faith so that grace by their efforts does not corrupt their belief in God's overcoming power for victory.

Some will ask why the author talks so much about evangelism and doctrinal correctness when the subheading reads; The House Church Must Produce Leaders. Maturity is essential for all Christian people. Making disciples is about teaching Christian doctrine and making it meaningful for living. As all grow in Christ to maturity, the older women teach, the younger, and the men can become elders and pastors of other house churches.

What about seminary? The first Church turned the world upside down for Christ. They were, in large measure, unlearned men. Peter and John were Apostles, and what do you read about them in Acts 4:13, "Now as they observed the confidence of Peter and John and understood that they were uneducated and untrained men, they were amazed, and began to recognize them as having been with Jesus."

But they were Apostles; I can hear some saying. There is no worse argument to use when the Apostles as examples are said to be no example because they were Apostles. The Apostles are not examples when referring to Apostolic gifts as in 2 Corinthians 12; Paul states he had the signs of an Apostle. That is when people want them to be examples when they are not. The rest of the time, they are examples, even as Christ was. God took eleven men who were no bodies, uneducated, and untrained; here's the key, by the world's standards.

God does things differently. Human instructors teach the lesson, and they give a test. By acquiring intellectual facts, most things taught can be learned, or so the world believes. God puts people to the test, and then He teaches the lesson. The disciples were tested for three years, and having failed the test, they became Apostles. They learned the lesson at the cross, the resurrection, and the forty days following. On The Day of Pentecost, they received the Holy Spirit, were filled with unction and power, and by today's standards, were unqualified. Nevertheless, they did a far better job than we do.

House church leaders need to be discipled much like Christ discipled the eleven. An older leader who has studied the scriptures must spend much time helping younger converts grow in ability and humility. Leaders need to stay close to things that require a more experienced person. On-going discipleship is a New Testament pattern; see Paul and Timothy.

What qualifies a person to lead others to maturity is not a four-year degree of facts but devotion to God daily without relying on a degree. As an example of not depending upon a degree but God, I give Edward McKendree Bounds, born in northeastern Missouri on August 15, 1835. His legacy was not thousands of professing Christians, many of whom never exemplified a transformed life, as many do in America today, but eight volumes about prayer. His writings were not as a professor researching a subject but as a man searching for God in prayer.

Christians must learn how to war in the spirit. When Paul began his first letter to the Church at Corinth, an intellectual and very gifts church (chapter 1), one of his primary concerns was their fleshly living, as seen in Chapter 3:1, "And I, brethren, could not speak to you as to spiritual men, but as to men of flesh, as to infants in Christ."

There's nothing mature about an infant, so intelligence doesn't equal wisdom, and gifts do not equal maturity or Spirit-filled.

The Apostle Paul was a mature Christian man who was neither proud nor holding his confidence in his flesh or abilities, as seen in his third letter or 2 Corinthians 10:2-5, "I propose to be courageous against some, who regard us as if we walked according to the flesh. For though we walk in the flesh, we do not war according to the flesh, for the weapons of our warfare are not of the flesh, but divinely powerful for the destruction of fortresses. *We are* destroying speculations and every lofty thing raised up against the knowledge of God, and *we are* taking every thought captive to the obedience of Christ."

There can be no pride when someone places their confidence in divinely powerful weapons. Don't miss it; divinely powerful is another way of saying, "It is not me but God who is waging war for my benefit and deliverance. The fact that he says, "We are destroying," and "We are taking every thought captive" means he's present and in the battle but knows the reality and truth of Psalm 91:7-10.

"A thousand may fall at your side and ten thousand at your right hand, b*ut* it shall not approach you. You will only look on with your eyes and see the recompense of the wicked. For you have made the LORD, my refuge, e*ven* the Most High, your dwelling place. No evil will befall you, nor will any plague come near your tent."

Did you catch it? God first says, "You have made the LORD," in the second person,  and then switches to the first person, "my refuge." making the relationship intensely personal, indeed intimate and a possession. Mere belief without intimacy does not make a Christian.

That is what Paul said of himself, under the inspiration of the Holy Spirit and in all humility. This faith is the qualification of an elder, not because it was taught in a classroom but learned during the trials of life. In the context of house church elders, we have Hebrews 13:5-7, "*Make sure that* your character is free from the love of money, being content with what you have; for He Himself has said, "I will never desert you, nor will I ever forsake you," so that we confidently say, "The LORD is my helper, I will not be afraid. What will man do to me?" Remember those who led you, who spoke the word of God to you; and considering the result of their conduct, imitate their faith."

No doubt, many good and humble men lead churches for nothing else than the glory of God and in obedience to Christ to go and make disciples. Nevertheless, the Hebrew writer has good reason for warning believers on their way to live for Christ and make disciples that they make sure their character is free from the love of money. It is impossible to encourage another to live by faith when you are living for and depending upon the security that money (in the eyes of the world) can bring.

When the learning disciple looks on to the pastor, perhaps working a secular job or not but supported by the congregation, something Paul was not eager to do, he places his heart's affections on money. It is often easier for the on-looker to see than the one corrupted by the love of money. The one leading the way to live should be acutely aware of God's warning, and in this case is Proverbs 23:5, "When you set your eyes on it, it is gone. For wealth certainly makes itself wings Like an eagle that flies toward the heavens."

Accountability was never meant to be like Catholic priests, who supposedly are at a higher level than all others in the Church. He hears sins, gives a person repetitious prayers, and they are again forgiven. The Bible teaches that all believers go to God, not for the forgiveness accomplished on the cross once and for all time, but for clearing a guilty conscience so they can again walk in the Spirit. There is no New Testament priesthood in the sense of a separated people for a particular call. Every believer has a personal call. The elder is not a person with a unique call;

he is older, more mature, and wiser according to his Biblical knowledge. That's all!

We see this in Paul's letter to the Galatians. Beginning in 5:24, "Now those who belong to Christ Jesus have crucified the flesh with its passions and desires." Evil desires when Christ died on the cross, the believer crucified them, by God's grace and intercessory work, when by faith they acknowledged their sin and inability to do anything about it and trust in Christ alone for forgiveness. Such people belong to Christ, but not before their rebirth and subsequent faith.

Paul follows the believer's one-time death with an admonition and warning. "If we live by the Spirit, let us also walk by the Spirit. Let us not become boastful, challenging one another, envying one another." "If we live by the Spirit..." means you are born again. The challenge is "...let us walk by the Spirit." There can be no walk without first the grace of God that alone saves. All elders, pastors, and leaders must be trained to teach this kind of solid doctrine while humbly making themselves equally accountable to the flock.

The flock, likewise, must only exalt elders to what they have attained—the more prominent a person's responsibilities, the greater their accountability. All the while, no elder, pastor, or shepherd must ever approach the place Jesus Christ has in the Church. By comparison to Christ, all members are just that - equals.

From the previous statements of accountability, Paul moves

on to further show the equality of all believers. "Brethren, even if anyone is caught in any trespass, you who are spiritual, restore such a one in a spirit of gentleness; *each one* looking to yourself, so that you too will not be tempted. Bear one another's burdens, and thereby fulfill the law of Christ." (Galatians 6:1).

"If anyone" includes all. There is no particular place for leaders because they are not the only ones on display in a house church. Everyone is! Therefore, when anyone is "caught in a trespass," who should restore such a one? "You who are spiritual." Who are the spiritual? First, the saved; second, they are walking as they are saved." In a typical church, there are those on stage with a clear testimony of Christianity, and there are the inconspicuous in the community of "Church" and only as accountable as they are willing to be. However, a loving membership will seek out those who prefer no accountability.

In the next section, the Apostle speaks of humility. "*Each one* looking to yourself, so that you too will not be tempted. Bear one another's burdens, and thereby fulfill the law of Christ." Tempted to do what? Judge with a haughty spirit, so he says, "looking to yourself." A humble person says to themself, "Except for the grace of God there I go."

At the end of this section, in verse ten, we read, "...do good to all people, and especially to those who are of the household of the faith." He could have used any number of metaphors, but he identifies believers in this context, especially to "the household of the faith." First, he identifies the household as a family, not a church building, which is more of an institution. Within the family, we are instructed to do good, especially to the household of the faith. In the New Testament, Family members are only those whose faith translates into a transformed life.

# A Final Word about the House Church

## 1. The Ministry of a Deacon

In the New Testament, men were designated to serve (diakonos or deacon) as servants. In the case of Stephen, he was chosen to serve food or wait on the widows who were being overlooked: notice who decided who would serve and the qualifications of a New Testament server.

'Now, at this time, while the disciples were increasing [in number], a complaint arose on the part of the Hellenistic [Jews] against the [native] Hebrews, because their widows were being overlooked in the daily serving [of food]. So the twelve summoned the congregation of the disciples and said, "It is not desirable for us to neglect the word of God in order to serve tables. "Therefore, brethren, select from among you seven men of good reputation, full of the Spirit and of wisdom, whom we may put in charge of this task. "But we will devote ourselves to prayer and to the ministry of the word." (Acts 6:1-4)

There are servants and teachers in this scene. One cannot teach what they do not know. Therefore, it was important for the Apostles to study the word of God. Those who were to serve were also to have had a good reputation, full of the Spirit and wisdom. No person lacking a spiritual rebirth can exhibit an authentic good reputation, the filling of the Spirit, and godly wisdom. Therefore, we could refer to Stephen and, no doubt, the others as well-saved men and authentic Christians.

## 2. The Ministry of the Congregation of Disciples

"The statement found approval with the whole congregation; and they chose Stephen, a man full of faith and of the Holy Spirit, and Philip, Prochorus, Nicanor, Timon, Parmenas and Nicolas, a proselyte from Antioch. And these they brought before the apostles; and after praying, they laid their hands on them." (Acts 6:5-6).

We are told the statement found approval with the whole congregation. Did the Apostles need the approval of all the congregation? As trustworthy men, they did not take their authority too lightly or in a heavy-handed manner. Therefore, they entrusted the decision to the congregation; take note it is the congregation of disciples. In the New Testament, there are only disciples of Christ. Any man who trains another man does so to follow Christ and never himself. A shepherd can say, as Paul did, follow me as I follow Christ. Such a statement clarifies that a disciple only follows another as far as they follow Christ. Any departure from following Christ demands a withdrawal from following the shepherd. It becomes the learner's responsibility to differentiate between following a human shepherd and the chief shepherd.

## 3. The Ministry of the Spirit and Power

How does an ordinary church member speak with such power and wisdom that the educated elite cannot refute his arguments?

"And Stephen, full of grace and power, was performing great wonders and signs among the people. But some men from what was called the Synagogue of the Freedmen, ...rose up and argued with Stephen. But they were unable to cope with the wisdom and the Spirit with which he was speaking." (Acts 6:8-9).

To be clear, Stephen did not speak in the flesh, which, if that were so, some could say it was his tenacity and brashness that caused his persecution and death. However, the presence of the wonders and signs by the power of God authenticated his being full of the Spirit and power.

Next, beginning with the call and promises to Abraham, Stephen clearly articulated the promise of the coming Messiah and the unbelief and hardened hearts and idolatries of the people of Israel. Much like Peter on the day of Pentecost, his words pricked the people's hearts, but this time, instead of asking what can we do, they rushed upon him and stoned him to death.

## 4. The Ministry of Church Houses

"But Saul [began] ravaging the church, entering house after house, and dragging off men and women, he would put them in prison." (Acts 8:3)

Once, I mentioned to a church elder about the church houses in the book of Acts, and he responded that the book of Acts is not a blueprint for the Church today. He further remarked that the whole New Testament had to be considered. My response to any such person who says such a thing about the Book of Acts would be first to prove it. The second problem with such a response is dismissing an entire Book as not applicable when it is one of five historical books of the New Testament: the four Gospels and The Acts of Jesus Christ through the Apostles, which focus on building the first Church by divine power. The response seems brash to me.

If the Old Testament account of Israel's negative behavior wandering in the wilderness was as Paul stated, "Now these things happened to them as an example, and they were written for our instruction, upon whom the ends of the ages have come." (1 Corinthians 10:11). How would the dynamics and faithfulness of the first Church of the New Testament not be a template for us today?

Furthermore, Church history tells a grim story of how the Church went wrong theologically and certainly its polity. Church structure has been disastrous for spreading the Gospel in many ways. Saul of Tarsus had to go from house to house because that's how the first Church met. The Temple was for evangelism, and all the sermons in the Book of Acts were evangelistic.

My dear reader, if you have become so accustomed to Church that you could never see any reason for doing it a different way (even if the Bible became clear that your way did not please Jesus Christ), then reading this or any other book will never be of any benefit to you. Please know that my prayers especially go with you.

www.ingramcontent.com/pod-product-compliance
Lightning Source LLC
Chambersburg PA
CBHW030924090426
42737CB00007B/311